Copyright © 2020 Ravi Chandran
Publisher: Books on Demand GmbH, Copenhagen, Denmark
Print: Books on Demand GmbH, Nordstedt, Germany
Cover and laylout: EZZENZ, Denmark
ISBN: 9788743028895

ACKNOWLEDGEMENTS

I want to first and foremost thank Almighty God, from whom all wisdom, knowledge and blessings flow.

Secondly, a special thanks to all seminar audiences worldwide, who have encouraged me time and again, to pen down these teachings and produce it in a book format.

Thirdly, I also take this opportunity to thank my natural and spiritual families, for granting me the time and space needed, to work on this book.

Finally, a heartfelt gratitude to Ulf Laursen for help with graphics and layout. John Ruolngul, Charles Muli, Tolulope Bamidele for proof reading and Prince Ravi for editing.

To God be the glory.

FOREWORD

I have taught the 7 Biblical Economic Principles in seminars worldwide. Due to requests from audiences, I pen down these teachings. This book is written with those audiences in mind, just as I would have been addressing them in a seminar. I hope and pray, that these teachings will continue to be a blessing to many more.

Let me be quick to point out that this book is not a 'get-rich-quick' formula. Rather, it is about seven tangible expressions of devotional worship by believers, responding to a Sovereign God, in a love relationship that is based in Spirit and in Truth. The focus throughout the entire book will be about our relationship with God the Father, in response to what Jesus did on the cross, as revealed to us by the Holy Spirit. The blessings that flows out of this relationship is a by-product to be received, and not a prime product to be focussed on.

Worship, in the days of our spiritual forefathers, involved among other things, some kind of animal, agricultural or material sacrifice, as an act of devotion. The purpose of the sacrifice was meant to make atonement for sins and reconciling relationships between God and men. In the Hebrew language, sin can be translated as either 'missing the mark' (sin), 'to break faith' (transgression) or as 'being crooked' (iniquity). From the Garden of Eden, God initiated a way for mankind to be reconciled back to God. In the New Testament, Jesus declared that He is the way, the truth and the life.

With the development of global economy, finance was used as a means of exchange, to purchase sacrificial items. Jesus Christ became the ultimate sacrifice, eliminating blood sacrifice, once and for all. The sacrifices of worship we offer today are symbolic, and in commemoration of His Great Sacrifice on the Cross of Calvary. Likewise, water baptism is symbolic of a believer uniting with Jesus in death, burial and resurrection. So does the elements of communion, the bread representing the Body of Christ and the cup representing the Blood of Christ's New Covenant.

I would like to state that I am not an economist, thus, I will not venture into the current global macro or microeconomics. It is vital to point out that the global economic principles and Biblical Economic Principles are not similar, but opposite, in most cases. However, as a theologian, and one who practices and teaches these principles, I will share 7 Biblical Economic Principles. The hope is that you will be inspired to practice them, as an act of devotional worship to God, in response to His love so lavished on us graciously, abundantly and generously.

The seven principles I am about to explore are independent of each other, yet, interrelated. It is common in Christian circles to hear the phrases 'tithe and offerings' mentioned simultaneously during financial contributions in a typical church gathering. There are much more in Scriptures, besides 'tithe and offerings', which are also independent principles. Each principle is not meant to be practiced mechanically, as a humanistic religious act, let alone manipulatively or under compulsion. Rather, they are meant to celebrate, confirm, and commemorate a covenant relationship between believers and their Maker.

Lastly, the principles put forth in this book are from The Holy Bible. No doubt, we will differ in their interpretations, based on our own theological or denominational backgrounds. It is not my intention to try and convince readers one way or the other. Instead, viewing God's Word as infallible, let us respond to it by faith, conviction and reverent devotion. This will yield undeniable blessings from God, which are meant to be shared with others.

Thus, where we disagree, let us choose to do so in an agreeable fashion. Most importantly, "How do these principles affect my private relationship with my Saviour?", should be the quest to be pursued. That is why, time and again, several thoughts are repeated, intentionally, as I teach in seminars. I hope and pray, that they will resonate in our spirits. Meanwhile, join me in this journey, to taste and see, that the Lord is Good.

Ravi Chandran

TABLE OF CONTENTS

CHAPTER 1

TITHE - RECOGNISING THE LORDSHIP OF JESUS

The tithe is simply a tenth of that which we possess or acquire. The tenth portion is paid or returned to God as an act of devotional worship. It is not a gift; it is due payment, as it is His sacred portion. The purpose of the tithe is for recognising the Lordship of God, and the stewardship of man. Thus, it is an act of devotional recognition, that everything we possess comes from the Lord and belongs to Him. "The earth is the Lord's, and everything in it, the world, and all who live in it; for he founded it on the seas and established it on the waters." (Psalm 24:1-2)

The tithe is demanded by God on the premise that He is the Creator, Ruler, Provider and sustains all creation to date and for eternity. Without the understanding of this principle of God's Lordship and man's stewardship, the tithe may seem optional. It is not meant to be a reluctant or compelling gift, but an obligatory ordinance. In reality, it is mandatory. The implication of this principle existed right from the Garden of Eden, when man was permitted to eat fruits of any tree in the garden, except of the tree knowledge of good and evil. While the tree of good and evil was not a tithe in itself, the underlying principle of not touching or taking something that belongs to God, remains. Failing to do so will result in disobedience, theft and spiritual death.

Genesis 2:15-17
15 The Lord God took the man and put him in the Garden of Eden to work it and take care of it.
16 And the Lord God commanded the man, "You are free to eat from any tree in the garden;
17 but you must not eat from the tree of the knowledge of good and evil, for when you eat from it you will certainly die."

1

The severity of eating of the fruit from the forbidden tree or the sacred portion was spiritual death and separation from God. Prior to the entrance of sin and disobedience, man was holy and not spiritually separated from God. There were blessings in obedience and constant fellowship with God. Disobedience only brought curses and separation from God. The command of not to eat of the tree of knowledge of good and evil was not a polite suggestion, it was a definite instruction. Though Adam created none of the trees, nor its fruits, he was made the chief steward of the garden and of all creation on earth. There was just one exception - the sacred portion or a symbol of the tithe. That solely belonged to God. God's Lordship and the servanthood of man's stewardship was established, until it was deliberately broken by mankind.

While Adam went about naming God's creation on earth, caretaking Eden, enjoying the help and companionship of Eve, it was inevitable that they would have passed by the forbidden tree many times. Not being able to partake of its fruits was a constant reminder of the sacred portion which belongs to God, and their rightful place as His created obedient servants. It is most likely that Adam and Eve must have had conversations about all creation, including the tree of knowledge of good and evil, among themselves and perhaps with God. They had a holy relationship with God and each other, in daily fellowship, communication, communion and divine love.

The tree of good and evil established the understanding of the relationship between mankind and God. Another interpretation of this relationship could be, 'I am a Loving Master', and you are my 'beloved steward'. In other words, I am the Lord your Creator and you are my beloved servant. The tree of knowledge of good and evil was an indication of the principle of the tithe. It was not merely a restraining order - it was a law to establish the rightful place of the Creator in one's life. One that history has proven time and again, a challenge for mankind.

In contemporary language - it states; Jesus is Lord and I am His devoted bondservant. Everything I have comes from Him, thus I do not touch but return the sacred portion which belongs to Him, in recognition of this principle. This moral principle existed way before the ceremonial laws of Moses and continued right down to the time of Jesus, as it still does today.

Genesis 3:1-7
¹ Now the serpent was more crafty than any of the wild animals the Lord God had made. He said to the woman, "Did God really say, 'You must not eat from any tree in the garden'?"
² The woman said to the serpent, "We may eat fruit from the trees in the garden,
³ but God did say, 'You must not eat fruit from the tree that is in the middle of the garden, and you must not touch it, or you will die.'"
⁴ "You will not certainly die," the serpent said to the woman.
⁵ "For God knows that when you eat from it your eyes will be opened, and you will be like God, knowing good and evil."
⁶ When the woman saw that the fruit of the tree was good for food and pleasing to the eye, and also desirable for gaining wisdom, she took some and ate it. She also gave some to her husband, who was with her, and he ate it.
⁷ Then the eyes of both of them were opened, and they realized they were naked; so they sewed fig leaves together and made coverings for themselves.

This sad passage of Scripture illustrates the fall of mankind into sin. The serpent deceived them into doubting the nature and character of God's love, protection and providence, into believing that their secret desires can be fulfilled through creation (the fruit) rather than the Creator. The devil called God a liar and sadly they took the bait - as many still do today. Jesus called the devil a liar and the father of all lies. (John 8:44) Inevitably, they succumbed to the lust of the eye, the lust of the flesh and the pride of life. (1 John 2:16) They ate of the forbidden tree and stole that which did not belong to them. Keeping the tithe for oneself is similar to what took place in the Garden of Eden - theft and banishment from paradise.

After the fall of Adam and Eve into sin, they were banished from the Garden of Eden, so that they should not eat of the Tree of Life and live as immortal sinners. That would have permanently separated them from God with no possibility of redemption, as it is with the devil and his angels. It is often overlooked, that the first sin was more than succumbing to the lust of the eye, lust of the flesh and the pride of life - it was disobedience of God's command and robbing Him of His sacred portion - an attempt to replace creation with the Creator. Moreover, it was an act of wanting to be like God, not His steward bondservant, but His equal. (Genesis 3:4) In Malachi, God called it robbery, when they took what belonged to Him. (Malachi 3:8) As the sacred portion belongs to God, so does the tithe.

As Adam and Eve used to have fellowship with God in the cool of the day, much communication must have transpired between them regarding all matters. These truths must have naturally been passed on to their children in their post-Eden days. It has always been common, from ancient of days, for parents to educate their children from past knowledge and experience. Bearing in mind, there were no formal schools in those days. The conversations between Adam, Eve and their children must have included their sinless days, and the situations and circumstances that led to their banishment from Eden. God's provisional redemption plan, with the symbolic sacrifice of an innocent animal (indicating Jesus' ultimate sacrifice), must have been taught to Cain and Abel. (Genesis 3:15;21)

God's loving kindness was demonstrated by preventing them from living as eternal sinners, should they have consumed the fruit from the Tree of Life in their fallen state. Moreover, the first bloodshed on the planet took place when God had an animal sacrificially killed, to make garments to cover their nakedness. This was a sign and symbol of Jesus, the innocent Lamb of God who will eventually be sacrificed, to cover the nakedness of the sins of the world. Only a sinless sacrifice can atone for the sin of mankind, to restore our broken relationship with God. Jesus became that Second Adam, who obeyed God to the point of death on a cross.

Cain and Abel must have been made to understand why they worshiped God by faith, while awaiting redemption, as an act of God's love, mercy and kindness. Their sacrificial worship was a sign and symbol, commemorating the Messiah who will ultimately be sacrificed, and His sinless blood be poured out on the cross, for redemption of mankind. By this time, Cain and Abel would have been clothed in animal skins themselves, and history must have been very close to their hearts while walking and working in these garments. These garments of skin were a stark reminder of their short, but sad history, with a glimmer of hope.

Adam must have also enlightened them about the Messianic Prophecy from God as to "he will crush your head, and you will strike his heel" (Genesis 3:15b), referring to Jesus' ultimate destruction of the deceptive devil and his angels. The devil continues to steal from, kill and destroy God's chosen ones. (John 10:10) However, our Loving Father gives us abundant life through Jesus Christ. Out of this redemptive plan came the symbolic sacrificial rituals commemorating God's amazing, and unfailing love for fallen mankind, whom He still loves. Therefore, every time an animal sacrifice was offered, it was a re-enactment of the entrance of sin, and God's providential mercy, forgiveness and impending ultimate redemption - a sacred act of devotional worship.

5

In that light, Cain and Abel brought articles of sacrifice, as a symbol which should denote their underlying devotion and relationship with God. However, as we read in Genesis 4:2-5, while Cain's offering was rejected, Abel's was accepted. A close examination of this passage will reveal several principles in operation - three in particular. We will discuss two of them in later chapters.

Genesis 4:2-5
² Later she gave birth to his brother Abel. Now Abel kept flocks, and Cain worked the soil.
³ In the course of time Cain brought some of the fruits of the soil as an offering to the Lord.
⁴ And Abel also brought an offering - fat portions from some of the firstborn of his flock. The Lord looked with favor on Abel and his offering,
⁵ but on Cain and his offering he did not look with favor. So Cain was very angry, and his face was downcast.

The Scriptures reveal that after a period of time, Cain brought some of the fruits of the soil. Notice that it states "some" and not firstfruits. We will discuss more about the principle of the firstfruits in a later chapter. However, Abel brought "fat portions from some of the firstborn of his flock". The fat belongs to God. (Leviticus 3:16) It represents the sacred portion. It also speaks of the tithe which belongs to God.

The firstborn speaks yet of another principle, which we will dwell on in a later chapter. Leviticus 3:16-17 says, "The priest shall burn them on the altar as a food offering, a pleasing aroma. All the fat is the Lord's. "'This is a lasting ordinance for the generations to come, wherever you live: You must not eat any fat or any blood.'" Leviticus 17:11 says, "For the life of a creature is in the blood, and I have given it to you to make atonement for yourselves on the altar; it is the blood that makes atonement for one's life."

Cain's offering was not firstfruits. It was some of the fruits. Thus, Cain's offering displeased God and was rejected, while Abel's offering pleased God and was accepted. Cain's offering is symbolic of manmade religion. When Jesus was in Gethsemane, He prayed, "Not my will but yours be done." (Luke 22:42) That is the walk of faith and obedience. On the contrary, disobedience says, 'Not Your will but mine be done.' There is a right way, the only way, which is the truth as expected by God. Proverbs 14:12 says, "There is a way that appears to be right, but in the end, it leads to death." Mankind continues to try and change, ignore or modify God's ways via religion. Religion is an alternative, conscience-soothing, self-therapy to try and please God, according to our own rules, rituals and regulations.

Restoring a devotional relationship with God is opposite to man's fabrication of religion. It is about admitting one's sins and acknowledging the need of repentance and redemption. In other words, to use a common phrase of today, it says, "God, I blew it! I need Your help to fix this. Please help me to know what I need to do." Religion, on the other hand, depends on man's ingenuity and not God's commands. Religion says, 'Let my will be done!' Divine relationship says, "Not my will but yours be done."

Jesus said, "I am the way, the truth and the life." (John 14:6) In other words, there is no true 'religion' besides Jesus' remedy to get back to God. Acts 4:12 says, "Salvation is found in no one else, for there is no other name under heaven given to mankind by which we must be saved." He became the only sinless sacrifice for mankind to purchase our redemption. Again, according to Proverbs 14:2, "There is a way that appears to be right, but in the end, it leads to death." Religion has the appearance of spiritual piety, dignity and discipline, but lacks godly life transforming power. Religion is based on the works on man's invention and imagination, while a genuine relationship with

The Almighty God is based on faith. Why? Because our fore-fathers Adam and Eve 'blew it' - BIG TIME, and God was merciful to them and their offspring - us.

Cain's manmade religion, based on the works of his sweat, toil and labour, was rejected by God. It was a 'good' idea, but not a 'God' idea. No manmade religion of any kind, form or shape can be accepted by The Almighty God, as the very DNA of fallen mankind is sinful. The very premise from which religion originates is corrupted. In other words, the software that runs the hardware has a virus. Sin cannot atone for sin, as it takes sinlessness to atone for sin. Thus, the sinless Lamb of God, Jesus, made a way, the only way, by which one can be received by God. This was the way of redemption provided by God Himself. An act of sacrificial love.

Abel simply followed the symbolism by faith, and therefore his offering was accepted. "By faith Abel brought God a better offering than Cain did. By faith he was commended as righteous, when God spoke well of his offerings. And by faith Abel still speaks, even though he is dead." (Hebrews 11:14) Abel demonstrated the Lordship of God over his life and flocks, while Cain disregarded that significance. What's worse, instead of repenting of his sin, he took matters into his own hands and murdered his brother. Matthew 5:21-22 says, "You have heard that it was said to the people long ago, 'You shall not murder, and anyone who murders will be subject to judgment.' But I tell you that anyone who is angry with a brother or sister will be subject to judgment. Again, anyone who says to a brother or sister, 'Raca,' is answerable to the court. And anyone who says, 'You fool!' will be in danger of the fire of hell."

Thus, the ultimate fruits of religion are robbing God, hatred, discord, jealousy, anger, fits of rage, violence and ultimately murder. The first born now became the first murderer on planet earth. Instead of following the path of life (Jesus), he chooses the path of death and destruction (the devil). Exactly what his 'father', the devil, wanted to do to God, as written in Isaiah 14:14: "I will ascend above the tops of the clouds; I will make myself like the Most High." In other words, "I will get rid of God and replace Him with myself!"

Genesis 14:18-20
18 Then Melchizedek king of Salem brought out bread and wine. He was priest of God Most High, 19 and he blessed Abram, saying, "Blessed be Abram by God Most High, Creator of heaven and earth.
20 And praise be to God Most High, who delivered your enemies into your hand." Then Abram gave him a tenth of everything.

In Genesis 14, we read of an intriguing story of a war of four kings against five kings in which Lot, Abraham's nephew, was taken captive due to living in the war zone. Abraham and his household were not yet a nation at this time. However, with just 318 trained men, Abraham defeated the four kings and returned with the booty, including his nephew Lot and his family. At this victory, the defeated kings came out to meet Abraham and a mysterious figure, Melchizedek, priest of God Most High, came out to bless him and serve him bread and wine, (memorial symbols of a covenant or the body and blood of Jesus), and Abraham paid him a tithe of his booty.

Melchizedek himself was a typology of Jesus as stated in Psalm 110:4, "The Lord has sworn and will not change his mind: "You are a priest forever, in the order of Melchizedek." The same is quoted again in Hebrews 5:6, "And he says in another place, "You are a priest forever, in the order of Melchizedek." Both verses speak of the Messiah, Jesus Christ. One can conclude that Abraham symbolically paid his tithe to Jesus, whom Melchizedek represented. As a matter of fact, when we pay our tithe today, we actually pay it to Jesus. It is a sobering thought, if we paused for a moment, and thought about it. Likewise, when Jesus broke bread and served wine to His disciples, calling it a New Covenant, it is in memory or what Melchizedek, representing Him, received from Abraham.

Abraham must have realised the enormity of his victory, with the possible repercussions involved in it, should there be a counterattack. This was literally a tribe defeating four Kings along with their armies. It must have dawned upon him that this was nothing less than a miracle from Almighty God. It was not humanly possible, and surely God had given him the victory. Thus, he acknowledged God by paying a tithe to the priest of God Most High. As the victory was from God, thus, only God could continuously protect him.

Again, due to a relational understanding, Abraham knew the tithe established his devotion to God Most High as Lord, and his place as mortal man, needing His covenanted protection. How else could a mere tribe been involved in such an enormous geopolitical warfare, and come out overwhelmingly victorious? For what mortal man can defeat four kings and their armies with 318 men, albeit well trained - unless a divine force was in play.

We read in Genesis 15:1, "After this, the word of the Lord came to Abram in a vision: "Do not be afraid, Abram. I am your shield, your very great reward." His faith and trust in God yielded blessings of protection and reward. Among others, Abraham also feared he would have no offspring to inherit his great wealth and carry on his legacy. Then the Lord cut an unconditional covenant with Abraham, not only to protect him, but also to make his offspring as numerous as the stars in heaven. Abraham believed God and it was credited to him as righteousness. (Gen 15:6)

Genesis 28:18-22

*¹⁸ Early the next morning Jacob took the stone he had placed
under his head and set it up as a pillar and poured oil on top
of it.*
*¹⁹ He called that place Bethel, though the city used to be
called Luz.*
*²⁰ Then Jacob made a vow, saying, "If God will be with me
and will watch over me on this journey I am taking and will
give me food to eat and clothes to wear*
*²¹ so that I return safely to my father's household, then the
Lord will be my God*
*²² and this stone that I have set up as a pillar will be God's
house, and of all that you give me I will give you a tenth."*

In Genesis 28, we read of the story of Jacob, who was fleeing
from his brother Esau, after stealing his brother's birth right.
Jacob was on his way to his uncle Laban. Jacob falls asleep
midway through his journey, and has a dream of a stairway to
heaven, with angels ascending and descending. Upon waking
up, Jacob initiates one of the pivotal events of his life: he en-
ters into a covenant with God. Now, running away from his
brother for fear of his wrath, with an uncertain future ahead, he
pledges to acknowledge the Lordship of God over his future,
by honouring to pay a tithe of all he will possess.

For Jacob, this was a life transforming moment. All the future challenges, blessings, sorrows and joyful events of his life,
boiled down to this pivotal encounter with God. The tithe established that tie between him and God. Indeed, God protected
him until his ripe old age, while rewarding him all along, notwithstanding the challenges he faced.

Malachi 3:6-12
*⁶ "I the Lord do not change. So you, the descendants of Ja-
cob, are not destroyed.*
*⁷ Ever since the time of your ancestors you have turned away
from my decrees and have not kept them. Return to me, and*

I will return to you," says the Lord Almighty. "But you ask, 'How are we to return?'

⁸ "Will a mere mortal rob God? Yet you rob me. "But you ask, 'How are we robbing you?'

"In tithes and offerings.

⁹ You are under a curse - your whole nation - because you are robbing me.

¹⁰ Bring the whole tithe into the storehouse, that there may be food in my house. Test me in this," says the Lord Almighty,

"and see if I will not throw open the floodgates of heaven and pour out so much blessing that there will not be room enough to store it.

¹¹ I will prevent pests from devouring your crops, and the vines in your fields will not drop their fruit before it is ripe," says the Lord Almighty.

¹² "Then all the nations will call you blessed, for yours will be a delightful land," says the Lord Almighty.

We read in Malachi about the complacency of the nation of Israel (decedents of Jacob). Previously, they were in captivity in Babylon due to their constant unrepentant sins. Returning to the Promised Land, they have become complacent, yet again, about their devotional worship towards God. God was still reaching out to them, referring to them as the descendants of Jacob, and stressing the point that His relational covenant has not changed. In fact, it was they who had changed. It is interesting to note here, that God used the name Jacob, meaning 'deceiver' instead the new name Israel, meaning 'Prince of God' or 'wrestles with God'. The issue here is that the nation unanimously had chosen to deceive God, by withholding their tithes and offerings, naturally rejecting His Lordship.

The main purpose for the people of God, not prospering, was due to the fact that they were robbing God. One has to pause here for a moment and sincerely ask this question: "Was God interested in the material tithe and offering (remembe-

12

ring He created all things), or was it the devotional relationship between His covenant people and Him, that He was after?" Knowing God, the latter is more in harmony with His nature and character.

God is not lacking anything as He is All Sufficient. The purpose of tithing was to re-establish a broken covenant relationship between God and fallen man, stemming way back from the Garden of Eden. Again, God does not need anything from mankind. It is an honour, and a privilege, that we are granted the opportunity to return to Him, what rightfully belongs to Him, in the first place. God is no debtor to man.

The two principles specifically stated by God were tithes and offerings. We will cover offerings in the next chapter but let us remain focused on tithe for now. God specifically stated that withholding the tithe from Him was equivalent to robbing Him! That was exactly what Adam and Eve did in the Garden of Eden – rob God. That was what Cain did – rob God. As children of God, let us understand that robbing God, by withholding the tithe, is equivalent to denying His Lordship over our life. It is literally taking God for granted.

That is what every believer in Christ who does not pay their tithe to God does today - rob God and take Him for granted. How could you expect to be blessed by God while still robbing Him? It is unacceptable by any means. That is not a loving, worshipful, reverent, devotional relationship - it is robbery and needs repentance.

We cannot treat God thus, and expect to be blessed individually, as a family, as a church or a nation. It is a thief who behaves like that, and we certainly know who that thief is. John 10:10 says, "The thief comes only to steal and kill and destroy; I have come that they may have life, and have it to the full." On the contrary, our God of love gives sacrificially. John 3:16 says,

"For God so loved the world that he gave his one and only Son, that whoever believes in him shall not perish but have eternal life." Let us follow God's example and not that of the devil.

Luke 18:9-12
⁹ To some who were confident of their own righteousness and looked down on everyone else, Jesus told this parable:
¹⁰ "Two men went up to the temple to pray, one a Pharisee and the other a tax collector.
¹¹ The Pharisee stood by himself and prayed: 'God, I thank you that I am not like other people-robbers, evildoers, adulterers - or even like this tax collector.
¹² I fast twice a week and give a tenth of all I get.'

Another danger of a complacent relationship with God is to simply practice the tithe as a religious law, while ignoring the overall principles of God's character, nature and principles. This was how the Pharisees, Sadducees and Teachers of the Law behaved in the times of Jesus. They paid their tithe, but it was not out of a reverent devotional relationship. It was more of a 'Cain-like' religion: "If I did this, you surely are 'obliged' to bless me, God!?!" We must avoid falling into such self-righteous hypocrisy.

Matthew 23:23-24
²³ "Woe to you, teachers of the law and Pharisees, you hypocrites! You give a tenth of your spices - mint, dill and cumin. But you have neglected the more important matters of the law - justice, mercy and faithfulness. You should have practiced the latter, without neglecting the former.
²⁴ You blind guides! You strain out a gnat but swallow a camel.

Jesus rebuked the hypocrisy of the teachers of the law of his time, for obeying the principle of the law of tithe, but neglecting the more important matters of the law, such as justice, mercy and faithfulness. His rebuke to them was not to stop tithing, but along with the tithe, to produce fruit in their character that reflects God's nature. This is stated in Micah 6:8, "He has shown you, O mortal, what is good. And what does the Lord require of you? To act justly and to love mercy and to walk humbly with your God."

Jesus was always practising God's principles as he taught his disciples to obey both the laws of the land (as in paying your taxes) and the laws of God (as paying your due to God). In Matthew 22:21, Jesus said, "Then he said to them, "So give back to Caesar what is Caesar's, and to God what is God's." True believers always obey both the Laws of God, and the laws of the land simultaneously. The only exception we see in Scriptures are when the Laws of the Land are in direct opposition to the Laws of God. (In Exodus, Daniel, Esther etc and Acts 4:19; 5:29)

As we have established that the tithe belongs to God, be faithful in paying or returning it to Him. Whether you pay your tithe weekly, monthly or yearly, do it out of a covenant devotional relationship with God, acknowledging His Lordship and your stewardship of His providence.

On the general matter of giving, Paul had a suggestion for the Corinthians: "Now about the collection for the Lord's people: Do what I told the Galatian churches to do. On the first day of every week, each one of you should set aside a sum of money in keeping with your income, saving it up, so that when I come no collections will have to be made." (1 Corinthians 16:1-2) Though this passage is not directly related to tithing, the practicality of the process should be observed.

Save up your gift, in anticipation to pay. We have many forms of savings in our private economy. Perhaps, it is time to start saving up that which belongs to God, so we can duly pay the tithe. There are those who say, "I cannot afford to pay my tithe." To them, my response is, "You cannot afford, not to pay your tithe!" If we can afford to pay our tax, rent, mortgage, utilities, food, transport, education, entertainment and perhaps mobile device bills, we certainly can prioritise the tithe which is above and beyond these. You see, it is really a matter of priorities. Give to Caesar what belongs to him and to God what belongs to Him.

In Malachi 3:10, it says, "Bring the whole tithe into the storehouse, that there may be food in my house. Test me in this," says the Lord Almighty, "and see if I will not throw open the floodgates of heaven and pour out so much blessing that there will not be room enough to store it." As the storehouse was in the Temple, our 'storehouse' today is our local congregations, where we go and receive our spiritual food, nourishment, care and engage in involvement. We are exhorted in the Bible not to forsake the assembly of the saints. (Hebrews 10:25) Your local congregation should be your 'storehouse', where you invest time and resources, while receiving spiritual covering, leadership and shepherding. Matthew 6:21 says, "For where your treasure is, there your heart will be also." Please note that it is the believers who should support the local congregations, not the unbelievers.

Your tithe should not be 'designated' for other purposes, as in alms, which will be covered in a later chapter. It belongs to God and should be paid to your local congregation. Your local congregation is the spiritual family you are attached to, and accountable to. This could be your home-based church, where you regularly attend, or an extended church, that you attend while on long term travel, work or educational assignments. What the leadership of the church does with that money is solely their responsibility, and between them and God. God will hold every church leadership responsible and accountable, as to how they manage His finances. As far as our private accountability to God goes, while the tithe is in our possession, we are accountable for it. When delivered to the local church, they are accountable for it.

Finally, the popular argument that the principle of tithe was 'under the law' and we are now 'under grace' is null and void. As pointed out above, this principle existed way before the law of Moses, and continued right down to the time of Jesus. We must understand that there are Moral Laws and Ceremonial Laws. The Moral Code, as in the Ten Commandments, exists till today. The Ceremonial Code, a shadow of the Messiah, who became our Passover Lamb, ceased on the Cross of Calvary. Its objective was completed, as Jesus finished the work. Therefore, we do not offer animal sacrifices anymore. However, the symbolic meaning of Lordship, has not changed.

Thus, your tithing establishes the Lordship of Jesus, and your bondservant stewardship towards Him. We pay, or return our tithe to God, as it belongs to Him. Not doing so is robbing God and depriving ourselves of His blessings.

Last but not least, there are those who ask, "Should I tithe from my gross income or net income?" This has always been my reply, "Do you want gross blessings or net blessings?" It is strange how we pay taxes from our gross income, but when it comes to God, we seek a 'discount'. Let us all grow and mature in our relationship with God. Maturity and wisdom will be your guide. In short, paying our tithes is basically recognising the Lordship of Jesus.

CHAPTER 2

OFFERINGS - RECOGNISING THE WORK OF JESUS

The principle of offerings, unlike tithe, is an opportunity to freely bring a gift of love and gratitude to God, to commemorate His work. In fact, the Bible states that during the feasts where God's people appeared before Him, they were not to appear before Him empty-handed. "Three times a year all your men must appear before the LORD your God at the place he will choose: at the Festival of Unleavened Bread, the Festival of Weeks and the Festival of Tabernacles. No one should appear before the LORD empty-handed." (Deuteronomy 16:16)

Indeed, these verses refer to the ceremonial law and specific feasts. However, the principle God is stating should not be overlooked. Do not appear before God "empty-handed". In Christ, this principle refers to all believers, male or female as we are all one in Him. Besides, Proverbs 18:16 says, "A gift opens the way and ushers the giver into the presence of the great."

Our God who made the heavens and the earth, needs nothing from mankind. He is All Sufficient. (Acts 17:25) The purpose for bringing an offering to Him, is to understand and practice the principle of return. The principle of return functions as such that, you first give, then it will be given to you. You first sow, then you reap. That's why Jesus said it is more blessed to give, than to receive, as the giver will have a constant divine supply.

In the case of offerings today, this should be specifically meant to support His work on earth, the church of Jesus Christ. Jesus said, it is He who is building His church. (Matthew 16:18) The focal point is that God needs nothing from us, but it is an honour and privilege to be able to bring Him a gift. Our giving

19

opens a door to receive blessings from God. These blessings are multifaceted: spiritual, psychological, physical, emotional, material, natural, etc. Thus, we should not appear before the House of God or His church empty handed.

This principle is practiced in many cultures around the world, to honour, keep and maintain human relationships. In my culture, for example, it is normal to bring a symbolic gift such as a bouquet of flowers or some fruits, when visiting friends or family. Growing up as an unbeliever, my mother taught me to never visit others without bringing a symbolic gift. Perhaps, unknowing to her, this principle originated from the Biblical concept of not appearing before God "empty-handed".

God challenged us in Malachi to bring the tithes and offerings to His house, in order for him to open the windows of heavens to pour out blessings towards us. Our tithes prepare an open heaven of blessing for us. Our offerings determine the returned portion. Thus, we are taught the general principle of giving. Luke 6:38 says, "Give, and it will be given to you. A good measure, pressed down, shaken together and running over, will be poured into your lap. For with the measure you use, it will be measured to you." In context, this verse was written in connection with judging others. The principle of return should not be overlooked. According to the measure you use, it will be measured to you. This works for everything else in life: we reap what we sow.

When giving offerings in a church, it should never be mistaken with 'tipping' the 'performers'. We tip in a restaurant, theatre or for some services provided by men for our leisure. That is an act of alms, which we will discuss later. However, our offerings are not meant for the services we receive in the house of God, but rather to support the Work of God in its totality. Offerings are intentional support of Jesus' Works past, present and future. Due to the nature of God, He will open a divine window of blessings upon our life, for that recognition.

Thus, when we pay our tithe to God, we acknowledge His Lordship. In reality, we have given him nothing. It was due payment as discussed in previous chapter. We simply returned what belonged to Him. However, when we give our offerings to God, the windows of heaven are opened to us, for an outpouring of blessings, according to the measure we use. The only factor limiting the measure of blessings we receive is determined by our own measure used. According to the measure you use; it will be measured to you. Therefore, generosity is encouraged in offerings, and in the words of Jesus Himself, "It is more blessed to give than to receive." (Acts 20:35b)

The Bible describes seven types of offerings stated in the Old Testament. Notice that in all seven instances, it cost the worshipper something, notwithstanding that all that one possesses comes from God. A closer observation of these offerings indicates relational implications. These were meant to foreshadow the sacrificial work to be accomplished by the Messiah, through whom we have a covenant devotional relationship with God Almighty.

In other words, each offering is a commemoration of our devotional relationship with God for His ongoing work, for the cost He bore, and the reciprocation bestowed upon us. Again, it is a relational devotion, not an economic return. As the tithe acknowledges the Lordship of God in our life, each time we appear before God with an offering, not empty-handed, we celebrate our ongoing relationship with Him and the work He did, is doing, and about to do. We do this in response to His unfailing love and mercy towards us, and the cost He bore for our redemption. (Lamentations 3:22-23)

In Leviticus 1, we learn about the **burnt offering**, which purpose was for the atonement of sin. This offering was symbolic

21

of the atonement the Lord would obtain for our sins on the Cross. This was the earliest type of offering recorded in Scriptures, right from the Garden of Eden, as an innocent animal was sacrificed to make coverings of skin for Adam and Eve's nakedness due to sin. Abel, Noah, Job and others followed this divine pattern for offerings. The offering is meant to restore a broken relationship with God, for the forgiveness of our sins. This was done in acknowledgement, that an innocent blood (Jesus) would be sacrificed, to restore the broken relationship with God due to sin.

Scriptures point out that sin is breaking the Law or knowing what is right and not doing it. (1 John 3:4; James 4:17) We need to be aware that there are 3 aspects to sin. One aspect of sin is 'missing the mark' or falling short of God's will. A second aspect is transgression, or not being true to your word, as in breaking someone's trust. The third aspect is 'iniquity', which is essentially being crooked, or totally ingenuine. The offering of an innocent blood is to rectify missing the mark, breaking trust (in this case with God), and crookedness, which leads to contempt of the Person, Word and Ways of God.

Today, we ask God for forgiveness for our sins by faith, in the Blood of Jesus, which was poured out on Calvary for us. Thus, we respond to Him with an offering in thanksgiving of that holy fact. This should not to be mistaken as 'purchasing' our salvation or forgiveness. Salvation cannot be bought, let alone earned. It is a free gift from God (though it cost Him His Son), received by faith. Rather, the offering is a loving and tangible response that comes from a worshipper's heart of love and gratitude. It is a devotional love response.

In Leviticus 2, we learn about the **grain offering**. Its purpose was to express devotion to God for His faithfulness, goodness and providence. This offering was symbolic for a believer to reinforce his or her fellowship with God, which is never meant to be taken for granted. Today, we should worship and fellowship with God in spirit and in truth, daily, by reading his word, meditating on it, praying, taking communion, singing praises, and proclaiming His salvation to the lost.

In Leviticus 3, we learn about the **fellowship offering**, also known as the peace offering. Its purpose was for people or parties to make a covenant with each other, wanting the best for both parties' future. When Jesus broke the bread and served the wine at the Passover meal with His disciples, it was an invitation into the New Covenant - a peace covenant. (John 14:27) He paid for it with his blood on the cross. He wanted that covenant to serve as a memorial (yet another principle, which will be discussed later).

When we make a fellowship offering with God, it is in recognition that Jesus is the Way, the Truth and the Life. "Salvation is found in no one else, for there is no other name under heaven given to mankind by which we must be saved." (Acts 4:12) The peace He gives us is not like that of the world. His peace means, in the midst of trouble, we remain peaceful and steadfast. (John 14:27)

In that light, we have been entrusted a ministry of reconciliation, to reconcile man to God. "All this is from God, who reconciled us to himself through Christ and gave us the ministry of reconciliation: that God was reconciling the world to himself in Christ, not counting people's sins against them. And he has committed to us the message of reconciliation." (2 Corinthians 5:18-19) Reconciling man with God begins with reconciling man with man. How can we say we love God, while we hate His images - mankind. 1 John 4:20 says, "Whoever claims to love God yet hates a brother or sister is a liar. For whoever does not love their brother and sister, whom they have seen, cannot love God, whom they have not seen."

We must love God with all our heart, mind, soul and strength, and our neighbours as ourselves. (Luke 10:27) Blessed are the peace makers, not the peace lovers. (Matthew 5:9) There are those who love peace. While it may not cost us anything to 'love' peace, it certainly costs to 'make' peace. It costs, even at the expense of being misunderstood, abused or persecuted. The question is: "Will we pay the price?" The ministry of reconciliation has a price to be paid. Jesus paid the ultimate price.

In Leviticus 4:1-35; 5:1-13, we learn about the **sin offering**. Its purpose was to remove the guilt of sins committed unintentionally. The Lord taught His disciples to pray daily for the forgiveness of sins. "And forgive us our debts, as we also have forgiven our debtors." (Matthew 6:12) Notice, the Lord is not only concerned about our relationship with Him, but also about our relationship with each other. In fact, we are told "For if you forgive other people when they sin against you, your heavenly Father will also forgive you. But if you do not forgive others their sins, your Father will not forgive your sins." (Matthew 6:14-15) As we pray for daily forgiveness of unintentional sins of our own, notwithstanding the intentional ones, so must we forgive those who unintentionally sin against us, even if it was intentional.

Again, "Therefore, if you are offering your gift at the altar and there remember that your brother or sister has something against you, leave your gift there in front of the altar. First go and be reconciled to them; then come and offer your gift." (Matthew 5:23-24) It is vital to God that our love relationship with Him is not only about us and Him, but also about us and others. "And you shall love the Lord your God with all your heart, with all your soul, with all your mind, and with all your strength.' This *is* the first commandment. And the second, like it, is this: 'You shall love your neighbour as yourself.' There is no other commandment greater than these." (Mark 12:30-31)

As much as we seek and desire God to forgive us of our sins daily, so must we search our hearts and forgive those who sin against us. This is inevitable - sinners saved by grace, and sinners unsaved, will sin against us daily. We must find it in our hearts to let go, and let God be the judge.

In Leviticus 5:14-19; 6:1-7, we learn about the **guilt offering**, also known as the trespass or reparation offering. Its purpose was to pay a penalty or debt, for the consequences of one's sins, with the desire to make right. To trespass is to break trust, particularly in a trusted or covenanted relationship. Interestingly, this offering could be paid in silver or a ram.

Today, Jesus is our High Priest, and the Prince of Peace helps us break down every wall of condemnation and leads us to Godly conviction that produces repentance. "For He Himself is our peace, who has made both one, and has broken down the middle wall of separation," (Ephesians 2:14) "For godly sorrow produces repentance leading to salvation, not to be regretted; but the sorrow of the world produces death." (2 Corinthians 7:10)

When a woman was caught in the act of adultery and brought to Jesus, the Law of Moses stated she should be stoned to death. Jesus however asked the crowds that those without sin, should cast the first stone. (John 8:1-11) The crowds left, from oldest to youngest, after this appeal. Jesus not only forgave her but told her to "go and sin no more". True repentance is not only feeling bad about what we have done, let alone being caught in the act. True repentance is a determination to change one's mind and actions, for divine life transformation, which comes through repentance.

In Leviticus 22:17-21, we learn about the **freewill offering**, also known as the "thank offering" or one brought to God in fulfilment of a vow. This offering can be brought at any time of the year and not necessarily in conjunction with a specific feast. In construction of the Tabernacle, God instructed Moses in Exodus 25:2, "Tell the Israelites to bring me an offering. You are to receive the offering for me from everyone whose heart prompts them to give." The key element here is "whose heart prompts them". Likewise, in construction of the Temple as written in 1 Chronicles 29:1-9, we read of the freewill offerings of David and the elders. They gave sacrificially, which is yet another principle, to be discussed later.

"Through Jesus, therefore, let us continually offer to God a sacrifice of praise - the fruit of lips that openly profess his name." (Hebrews 13:15) The **sacrifice of praise** is yet another form of offering to God. Once again, this offering is meant to reinforce, publicise and celebrate our relationship with Jesus. It is also worth mentioning that, praise is not necessarily something we offer when we 'feel' good. There are difficult times in life, where one offers praise, as a sacrifice, and in faith, while still in the midst of trouble. Those who sow in tears will reap with joy. (Psalm 126:5-6) Scriptures encourage everything that has breath, to praise God. (Psalms 150:6) Let us praise Him, not only in good times, but especially in challenging ones.

In all the examples given by Scriptures concerning bringing an offering to God, the implication always boils down to amending, or mending a relationship, either with God or men. Each offering costs the worshipper something, although, all he or she has come from God. The general idea that the children of Israel were taught, was to never appear before God empty-handed. In fact, they would not appear before a prophet, or a man of God, empty-handed. This was solely because they always associated the man of God with the work and voice of God.

This should always be the case, though today, not everyone who associates himself or herself with God, is necessarily called, let alone sent by God. (Matthew 7:15-20) In Biblical times, if one was found out to be a false prophet, he or she would be stoned to death. If that same principle were applied today, we would probably have less false prophets. There are many who call themselves a prophet or a man of God. It is up to the reader to discern the truth. However, Jesus left us with the Holy Spirit to teach us all truth and give us discernment. (John 16:13; 1 Corinthians 12:10)

When his father's donkeys were lost, Saul's servant wanted him to inquire from prophet Samuel about it. Saul hesitated, as he had no gift to bring to him. "Saul said to his servant, "If we go, what can we give the man? The food in our sacks is gone. We have no gift to take to the man of God. What do we have?" The servant answered him again. "Look," he said, "I have a quarter of a shekel of silver. I will give it to the man of God so that he will tell us what way to take." (1 Samuel 9:7-8) The notion to not appear before a man of God empty-handed, was derived from not appearing before God empty-handed.

Today, we do not bring offerings of animals or otherwise to God, as Jesus has become the ultimate sacrifice for us all. Instead, we offer a symbolic substance, or the cost of an offering, above and beyond our tithes, to bless His house and support His work – the church of Jesus Christ. Jesus said, He is the builder of the church. Thus, when we bring our offerings to the church, in reality, we bring them to Jesus. "So I tell you, you are Peter. On this rock I will build my church, and the power of death will not be able to defeat it." (Matthew 16:18) Bringing our finances, time, service, support, talents, and sacrifice to the church, is one of the greatest forms of helping Jesus build His work.

Often believers overlook that it takes finances to pay the rent, mortgage, utilities, payroll, logistics, transport, equipment, maintenance, and ongoing expenses of a church. It is not the unbelievers that are going to donate to this course. It has to be the believers, who bear that load. If each believer understood this vital role, and gave generously to their local congregations, the house of God would never be in need. Sadly, many people look at offerings as an act of charity, rather than a gift of love. This calls for a devotional relational understanding, of what it means to build alongside with Jesus, and support His ministry and ministers.

It is important to point out that God always meets the needs of His work - with or without believers. Thus, it is an honour and privilege for believers to participate in this process, and be blessed, besides being a blessing. However, God can use anyone or anything, if He so desires. He would even use a raven to feed a prophet, if that is what it takes. (1 Kings 17:2-16)

When we bring our offerings to God, we should not do it because we have to, but we should do it because we want to, due to our devotional love for Him. Our attitude and motive for giving offerings must be one of devotional love and thanksgiving. When Jesus sent out his disciples to preach the gospel, he admonished them, "freely you have received, freely give." (Matthew 10:5-8)

Similarly, everything we are, and have, is from God. He lavished His abundant blessings and love on us. Therefore, when we offer our offerings to Him, let us do it freely, cheerfully, willingly, not under compulsion or guilt, but out of a genuine devotional love for Jesus, to build His church. Giving our offerings is basically recognising the Work of Jesus.

CHAPTER 3

ALMS - RECOGNISING THE KINDNESS OF JESUS

The alms are also known as charitable deeds, acts of righteousness, giving to the needy or donations. This act of kindness is above and beyond one's tithe and offerings. When we pay our tithe, we return, or pay God, what belongs and is due to Him. When we offer our offerings, it is an expression of our devotional love and thanksgiving, a desire to support and build His ministry and work. Thus, the tithe and offerings are specifically meant for the house of God, or the church.

The alms, on the other hand, is a specific act of charitable kindness, in or out of the house of God. This may be practiced anywhere, when a believer feels a prompting in his or her heart, to help another person (in the church or in the world) tangibly, physically, financially, materially, psychologically, spiritually or where otherwise appropriate. An important factor of the alms is that, it should be practiced in confidentiality.

Matthew 6:1-4
¹ "Be careful not to practice your righteousness in front of others to be seen by them. If you do, you will have no reward from your Father in heaven.
² "So when you give to the needy, do not announce it with trumpets, as the hypocrites do in the synagogues and on the streets, to be honored by others. Truly I tell you, they have received their reward in full.
³ But when you give to the needy, do not let your left hand know what your right hand is doing,
⁴ so that your giving may be in secret. Then your Father, who sees what is done in secret, will reward you.

It is possible, when one does a charitable act, that it is publicised, and the giver receives a sense of admiration and applause.

According to Jesus, that was giver's "reward in full". However, He tells us not to follow that example, while practising our charitable deeds. He wants it to be done in privacy and confidentiality. The reason for this, when done so, will bring glory and honour to God. The instrument (donor) however, will be rewarded by God Himself.

It was common to have the poor and needy begging for food, money or practical assistance in the streets of Jerusalem, and by the temple gates in particular, even in the times of Jesus. Today, we may have people begging in the streets of many contemporary cities. Jesus said, the poor, we will have with us always. (Matthew 26:11) I will point out later, the importance of not being manipulated into giving, out of guilt, feeding a greed, but to do so meeting genuine needs. Jesus taught us to meet needs and not to feed greed when he said, "give to the needy" be it in the 'synagogue' (church where appropriate) or 'streets' (world where appropriate). It should be done in discretion, anonymity and without publicity.

Acts 3:1-10
¹ One day Peter and John were going up to the temple at the time of prayer - at three in the afternoon.
² Now a man who was lame from birth was being carried to the temple gate called Beautiful, where he was put every day to beg from those going into the temple courts.
³ When he saw Peter and John about to enter, he asked them for money.
⁴ Peter looked straight at him, as did John. Then Peter said, "Look at us!"
⁵ So the man gave them his attention, expecting to get something from them.
⁶ Then Peter said, "Silver or gold I do not have, but what I do have I give you. In the name of Jesus Christ of Nazareth, walk."
⁷ Taking him by the right hand, he helped him up, and instant-

ly the man's feet and ankles became strong.
⁸ He jumped to his feet and began to walk. Then he went with
them into the temple courts, walking and jumping, and prais-
ing God.
⁹ When all the people saw him walking and praising God,
¹⁰ they recognized him as the same man who used to sit beg-
ging at the temple gate called Beautiful, and they were filled
with wonder and amazement at what had happened to him.

The man begging by the temple, knew that charitable deeds
was taught in the Scriptures. Thus, what better place to be at,
rather than the temple gates. Perhaps, people were in a more
'generous' mood to part with some gift, after worshipping
God. In this particular occasion however, he got a little more
than what he begged for - he got total healing and was able to
walk and work again!

Though this book is not about healing, notice that Peter and
John actually stopped to converse with the beggar, and paid
attention to his genuine appeal. Perhaps, if they had silver
or gold, they might have parted with it. However, they gave
him something more precious - healing by the Name of Jesus
Christ of Nazareth. The ultimate act of generosity is to deliver
one from the source of all poverty and see them set free in the
Name of Jesus. No doubt, this man will never ever need to beg
again! He would from then on, be able to work with his own
hands and earn a decent, and honourable living. What a gift he
received!

We are taught in Scriptures to be kind and generous. Proverbs
19:17 states, "Whoever is kind to the poor lends to the Lord,
and he will reward them for what they have done." Kindness is
often expressed beyond words of encouragement and goes into
practicality, and tangible deeds within one's means and ability.
James 2:16 says "Suppose a brother or a sister is without clothes and daily food. If one of you says to them, "Go in peace;

keep warm and well fed," but does nothing about their physical needs, what good is it?" This is a practical example, or faith and action working hand in hand.

Notice, when you are kind to the poor, you lend to the Lord! What an honour and privilege! God owns everything and has need for nothing. Knowing, God is no debtor to any man, "lending" to Him simply equates to "storing up treasures in heaven". Besides, God promises that you will be rewarded, both in heaven and while on earth. (Mark 10:29-31) Our motive to be kind and generous should not be for the sake of seeking rewards, or storing up treasures, but rather to be an expression of Jesus' kindness. However, it is comforting to know God sees, what is done in secret and rewards us, as is His nature.

Proverbs 21:13 states, "Whoever shuts their ears to the cry of the poor will also cry out and not be answered." God is concerned for the poor and needy. If their cry is within our ability to act, react or help, be quick to respond. Deliberately ignoring their voice, may result in our voice not being heard by God, when we are in need. This is a solemn warning from The Word of God. Therefore, if it is within your ability to show an act of kindness, do not procrastinate.

One may pose a logical question regarding the poor: "Why not simply eliminate poverty altogether?" Technically speaking, the world has more than enough supply to meet every need. The question of poverty is beyond economic principles of demand and supply, it goes into management of the supply and demand. Often, selfish men hoard supplies to inflate prices, especially during a time a great demand. (Proverbs 11:26)

Again, I am not an economist so I will avoid entering into that discussion. However, Jesus did say, "The poor you will always have with you." (Matthew 26:11a) Thus, rather than being overwhelmed with the poverty that exists in the world and around you, simply do your part to help relief it, within your ability.

When giving to the poor and needy, do your best to ensure that the needs presented are genuine. It is unfortunate that not all 'needs' are genuine nor authentic, let alone, credible. You must distinguish the difference between, meeting a need and feeding a greed. While the former is a noble cause, the latter could be a deceptive scheme, plotted by selfish men, whose main purpose is to take advantage of your generosity. There are many scams in this wicked world, especially targeted towards the innocent, kind and generous. While believers are expected to be innocent as a dove, they are also admonished to be shrewd as a serpent. (Matthew 10:16) Be vigilant while practicing generosity.

There are many credible and reputable charitable organisations, doing a great deal of good to help the poor and needy. Sadly, there are also those whose ulterior motives are to profit from another's despair. This is especially true when solicited via bogus e-mails or unverified websites. When donating to a charitable cause via third party organisations, do a little research into the organisation. Ensure that what you give goes towards the advocated purposes, and not into large administrative fee, to sustain the donor organisation.

Remember, we are sent forth as sheep among wolves. Thus, ensure that your generosity is not taken advantage of, or manipulated, by professional scammers. Sadly, time and again, the generosity of mankind is abused by dubious characters and suspect organisations.

Ensure that when you are practicing an act of charity, it is done so because of your conviction, based on the Word of God, rather than a feeling of 'guilt'. Guilt based giving is not sustainable, let alone Biblical, and only leaves you feeling used and manipulated. Conviction based giving is Biblical, leaves you with a sense of being an extension of the kindness of Jesus, resulting in peace, joy and a sense of fulfilment.

If one manipulates you into charity by guilt-based, fundraising schemes, the need will have to be exaggerated time and again, to get a response from you. The newsletters multiply, the images of the needy gets more graphic, and the urgency is emphasized to trigger an immediate response. Some believers genuinely need to be set free from such strongholds of persons, or organisations, who abuse genuine kindness to gratify a never ending 'need'.

Our charitable acts could be gifts given towards church planting, missionaries, specific fundraising programs in a church, for a targeted project, charitable organisations, disaster relief, a stranger or person who is in genuine need. It may involve giving a generous tip for a service you received. The possibilities of showing financial, material and emotional kindness are endless. There will always be needs present.

Always ensure that your charity is done genuinely, with no intent to draw attention to yourself, not feeding a greed, but meeting a need, and to be an extension of Jesus' kindness. We will not always get it right, and perhaps, more than once, fall into a wicked trap we did not anticipate. However, with time, God will help us to practice our alms in a way that pleases Him. We will be rewarded, among other things, with a gift of discernment.

Again, we must bear in mind that giving to charity is above and beyond our tithe and offerings. Your tithe belongs to God. He deserves your offerings. Your charity is an extension of the kindness of Jesus. Thus, you cannot designate your tithe nor your offerings towards charity. That would be robbing the sacred portion and placing it elsewhere or stealing what should be used for building the church of Jesus. Ensure that when you practice charity, the tithe and offerings are not neglected, let alone reassigned. As mentioned, your acts of kindness should be above and beyond your tithe and offerings. Principles of tithes, offerings and alms should not be confused.

Believers, among other things, should be the most generous people on this planet. The philosophy of this world is to get all you can get, place it all in a can, and sit on the can - which is the pinnacle of selfishness. Believers should be an expression of, give all you can, store up treasures in heaven, and sacrifice, if need be. We will discuss the principle of sacrifice, the ultimate giving, in the last chapter.

When you tap into the supernatural providence of God, the truth is, you will constantly be looking for opportunities to practice charity. God will lead you to hidden treasures in secret places so that you will continue be a channel of His endless blessings. (Isaiah 45:3) Proverbs 28:27 says, "Those who give to the poor will lack nothing, but those who close their eyes to them receive many curses." Let us choose to be a channel of blessing, not otherwise. Practicing alms is basically recognising the kindness of Jesus.

CHAPTER 4

FIRSTRUITS - RECOGNISING THE PRIORITY OF JESUS

The firstfruits or firstborn principle is recognising that Jesus is the firstborn of all creation and should have first priority in our life. The meaning of our existence is to prioritise God, worship Him, serve Him, and bring glory to Him in Jesus' Name. No other relationships, biological, emotional or otherwise should come between us and God. Jesus is Lord of all, or He is not Lord at all. We serve a jealous God. (Exodus 20:5)

Going back to Genesis, concerning the offerings brought by Cain and Abel, we noted that Cain brought "some of the fruits" (speaking of manmade religion) while Abel brought "fat portions" (speaking of the tithe) of the "firstborn" (speaking of Jesus) of his flock. Abel recognised, understood, and practiced the divine principle by faith, which made God favour his offering. Cain brought "some of the fruits" - not even the firstfruits - which caused his offering to be rejected.

As mentioned earlier, it is most likely that Adam would have educated Cain and Abel of the principles concerning firstfruits and all other redemptive principles of God. Until then, Adam was the wisest man who walked the surface of the earth. The information passed on to his children were first-hand accounts. However, Cain deliberately choose to disobey God. Even God questioned Him, "If you do what is right, will you not be accepted?".

He knew what was right but choose not to do it. Instead, he chooses to become angry with God and his brother. Genesis 4:6-7 states, "Then the Lord said to Cain, "Why are you angry? Why is your face downcast? If you do what is right, will you not be accepted? But if you do not do what is right, sin is crouching at your door; it desires to have you, but you must rule over it."

After the fall of Adam and Eve, when God prophesied about the Messiah as the "seed" and sacrificed an animal on their behalf, Adam must have known how fallen mankind should worship God and seek His grace, mercy, justice and ultimate salvation. Right there in the Garden of Eden, God took steps to demonstrate that His Firstborn, will pay the price for man's sin. The firstborn will come through the seed of Adam - Jesus Christ our Messiah. As mankind offered the firstborn of the womb, their flock or firstfruits of their harvest, it was an act of commemorating the symbol of what God had done, and ultimately will do, as Jesus fulfilled on the cross.

The only way this sacrifice could be destroyed, was by preventing Jesus from ever appearing on planet earth. The battle for the destruction of the Seed of God, prophesied in Genesis, continued throughout the ages from Noah's time with the flood, the attempted destruction of Moses and all male Hebrew boys during the time of his birth, the male children murdered by King Herod, and even Judas as inspired by the devil himself to betray Jesus.

Jesus is our firstfruit and firstborn who resurrected (as He covenanted), broke the bread representing His body, shared the wine representing His blood, and paid the ultimate sacrifice. It is thus appropriate that as often as we celebrate communion, we remember the work of the firstborn, the second Adam - Jesus Christ our Lord and His accomplishment of the work on the cross for us. Thus, as often as we partake the communion, we remember the Lord's death, burial, resurrection and soon coming. It is also a memorial which will be discussed later.

In Genesis 22, we read of the story of Abraham being tested by God, when Isaac was asked as a sacrifice. God knew that

He Himself would be offering Jesus, His own Son, in times to come for the forgiveness of mankind's sins. Although child sacrifice among pagan religions of that time was common, Abraham reasoned within himself that God could even raise the dead. (Hebrews 11:19)

Some scholars believe that it was on that mountain, that God shared His plan of redemption with Abraham. This can come as no surprise, as God considered Abraham His friend, and even foretold the destruction of Sodom and Gomorrah before it happened. That caused Abraham to intercede for his nephew, Lot and his family.

Isaac, being the rightful promised firstborn, was demanded by God as a sacrifice. Some may argue that Ismael, Hagar's son was the firstborn. Although he was technically the firstborn, it was not what God had intended, let alone promised. Isaac was the firstborn of the womb of Sarah – the promised son. This too is another indication, like Cain's offering, where Sarah 'invented' a 'religion' of her own, by taking matters into her own hands. Having's Hagar's son, only to be rejected by God, as the inheritor of the promise. Ismael was blessed too, but the promised blessings of the firstborn was upon Isaac. Thus, God tested Abraham by asking him to offer up his firstborn.

We cannot modify God's plan by our own design and expect Him to change His plan to suit ours. On the mountain, God Himself offered a ram to be sacrificed. God likewise provided that Ram in the form of Jesus Christ, on another mountain, Golgotha, to become our sacrifice. God's eternal plans cannot be thwarted by mankind, or the devil and his hosts. Until the end, every detail of God's plan will be fulfilled. Jesus said in Matthew 24:35, "Heaven and earth will pass away, but my words will never pass away."

Exodus 13:11-16

11 "After the Lord brings you into the land of the Canaanites and gives it to you, as he promised on oath to you and your ancestors,
12 you are to give over to the Lord the first offspring of every womb. All the firstborn males of your livestock belong to the Lord.
13 Redeem with a lamb every firstborn donkey, but if you do not redeem it, break its neck. Redeem every firstborn among your sons.
14 "In days to come, when your son asks you, 'What does this mean?' say to him, 'With a mighty hand the Lord brought us out of Egypt, out of the land of slavery.
15 When Pharaoh stubbornly refused to let us go, the Lord killed the firstborn of both people and animals in Egypt. This is why I sacrifice to the Lord the first male offspring of every womb and redeem each of my firstborn sons.'
16 And it will be like a sign on your hand and a symbol on your forehead that the Lord brought us out of Egypt with his mighty hand."

To redeem the firstborn among their sons, the worshippers would offer the price of redemption. This was only done for the firstborn sons. Each firstborn male was made aware that they were offered to the Lord and belonged to Him. The purpose of this commemoration was because God Himself offered us His firstborn. When the all the firstborn of Egypt were struck by the plague, it was the ultimate test that made Pharaoh relent and let the Israelites go.

No doubt, it must have been in his mind, what he did to the male children of the Israelites during the time of Moses, to have them slain. God defied all the ten major gods of Egypt, and made a humiliating spectacle of them, exalting His sovereign splendour and awesome power. Each plague that came on Egypt was a direct judgement on their gods and its followers. The children of Israel had to commemorate this for all time, by sacrificing all the firstborn of their animals, and setting aside all firstborn male child. Eventually, God Himself sacrificed His Firstborn Son, set aside for us.

Numbers 15:17-21
[17] The Lord said to Moses,
[18] "Speak to the Israelites and say to them: 'When you enter the land to which I am taking you [19] and you eat the food of the land, present a portion as an offering to the Lord.
[20] Present a loaf from the first of your ground meal and present it as an offering from the threshing floor.
[21] Throughout the generations to come you are to give this offering to the Lord from the first of your ground meal.

The above Scriptures states that they should not just present any loaf, but specifically a loaf made out of the first of their ground meal. Note, the emphasis on the first. This was no ordinary loaf; it was from the first ground meal. Thus, they offered to the Lord the first loaf, a symbol of the Messiah, the Firstborn. It speaks of Jesus Christ, having the first priority in our life. Again, not any loaf of bread, but the first. The first belongs to God – symbolic of the firstborn.

Deuteronomy 26:1-4
[1] When you have entered the land the Lord your God is giving you as an inheritance and have taken possession of it and settled in it,
[2] take some of the firstfruits of all that you produce from the soil of the land the Lord your God is giving you and put them in a basket. Then go to the place the Lord your God will choose as a dwelling for his Name
[3] and say to the priest in office at the time, "I declare today to the Lord your God that I have come to the land the Lord swore to our ancestors to give us."
[4] The priest shall take the basket from your hands and set it down in front of the altar of the Lord your God.

41

As believers, our 'Promised Land' is being delivered from a life of sin and bondage, into entering a life of righteousness, freedom and forgiveness in Christ Jesus. The dwelling place of God today is both the collective house of God (church) and our individual bodies (Temple of the Holy Spirit). Thus, God leads us to be part of a local church, while He Himself dwells within us, His temple. The priest is the shepherd or pastor of that church.

We should thus bring our firstfruits to the house of God (church), where He has settled us in. This should also give us a better understanding of the church of Jesus Christ. It is not a secular organisation but a spiritual organism. The house God choose as His dwelling place. Jesus said, "And I tell you that you are Peter, and on this rock I will build my church, and the gates of Hades will not overcome it." (Matthew 16:18)

Nehemiah 10:35-37
[35] "We also assume responsibility for bringing to the house of the Lord each year the firstfruits of our crops and of every fruit tree.
[36] "As it is also written in the Law, we will bring the firstborn of our sons and of our cattle, of our herds and of our flocks to the house of our God, to the priests ministering there.
[37] "Moreover, we will bring to the storerooms of the house of our God, to the priests, the first of our ground meal, of our grain offerings, of the fruit of all our trees and of our new wine and olive oil. And we will bring a tithe of our crops to the Levites, for it is the Levites who collect the tithes in all the towns where we work.

When the exiles of Israel returned to Jerusalem to rebuild the temple and the wall under the leadership of Ezra and Nehemiah, a selected group made a vow and bound themselves with a curse, to fully obey the Lord and follow His commandments. This was following their exile, due to constantly abandoning the laws and principles of God's Word. Among other things, one of their vows was to resume bringing to the house of God the annual firstfruits, without neglecting offering of the first-born sons, cattle and herds. It is vital to note that the firstborn sons were not meant to be sacrificed, but rather dedicated to God.

This was similar to the vow Hannah made before the birth of Samuel - to give him to the Lord. Note that this doesn't mean every first born should become a minister or a missionary. Today, all believers are counted among the firstborn. We all have been given the ministry of reconciliation. However, each firstborn of a household, male or female, should always be first in line, to offer any service that the house of God requires. Remember, though we all belong to God and are 'firstborns', you, the firstborn of the womb, have been symbolically set aside. Remember this the next time there is an appeal for help in the House of God.

Psalm 89:27 says, "And I will appoint him to be my firstborn, the most exalted of the kings of the earth." While this Psalm talks about King David, it also speaks prophetically of Jesus, the firstborn. Jesus is the image of the invisible God, the firstborn of all creation. (Colossians 1:15) God ordained that we who believe in Him, will be counted among the firstborn. This is an honour and a privilege.

Romans 8:29 says, "For those whom He foreknew, He also predestined to become conformed to the image of His Son, so that He would be the firstborn among many brethren;". It says in Revelation 1:4-5, "John, To the seven churches in the province of Asia: Grace and peace to you from him who is, and who was, and who is to come, and from the seven spirits before his throne, and from Jesus Christ, who is the faithful witness, the firstborn from the dead, and the ruler of the kings of the earth." Jesus, the Firstborn from the dead, resurrected to conquer sin and death so that in and through Him, we too will have life and resurrection.

It is appropriate to mention, that though the early church used to meet in the temple courts and from house to house, predominantly on the Sabbath, which is the seventh day of the week, they eventually moved their day of worship to the first day of the week - the day Jesus resurrected. Again, the principle of the first is observed here. When Jesus taught us to seek first His Kingdom, the emphasis was on the "first". Matthew 6:33, "But seek first his kingdom and his righteousness, and all these things will be given to you as well." This verse is popular and often quoted, but one vital word is often overlooked - "first".

Today, we can recognise this principle by many tokens. First, as most believers use a Gregorian calendar instead of a Jewish Calendar, try to set aside a portion of your first salary of the month, above and beyond your tithe, offerings and alms, as the 'firstfruit' gift to God. Do likewise with the first dividend or the year, business profit, extra income etc.

For those whose faith allows, when you receive your first official salary when employed, I challenge you to return the entire salary back to God. This is a test of faith. Only those who feel led to follow this test should do this. I am speaking from experience. Then see, how for the rest of your life, it will be jobs seeking you, rather than you seek jobs.

Taking it further, make it a priority on the first day of the week, Sunday, as a day dedicated to God. Make it a goal, never to miss Sunday services, wherever you are in the world – home-based or on assignment abroad. Be present in person, or online, where appropriate. Even while exiled on the Island of Patmos, John was "in the Spirit on the Lord's Day". (Revelation 1:10) Just think about this. A prisoner, abandoned, no church, yet "in the Spirit on the Lord's Day". What an inspiration!

Perhaps spend more time in prayer and fasting, the first day of each month. Try to spend the first month of the year dedicated to fasting and prayer, within the capacity and understanding of your ability. When you prioritise time for God, you will experience accomplishing more in the remaining 11 months, than you otherwise would be able to accomplish by human standards.

The principle of the first is to prioritise God above all. Jesus said, "No one can serve two masters. Either you will hate the one and love the other, or you will be devoted to the one and despise the other. You cannot serve both God and money." (Matthew 6:24) The principle of the first is to practically declare that God is first in your life, in words and deeds. The suggestions above are not 'rules or regulations' but creative ways to commemorate the principle of the first, in recognition of Jesus.

In the congregation I lead, each year we take time to pledge our firstfruit, by setting aside funds we call the 'New Year Pledge'. This amount is above and beyond our regular tithes, offerings, alms or otherwise. We teach the principle of the firstfruit and firstborn to the congregation and allow the Holy Spirit to convict those who want to participate, in free will. This has to do with a devotional relationship with God, and to apply faith, trust, and hope in Him.

Proverbs 3:5-10
⁵ Trust in the Lord with all your heart and lean not on your own understanding;
⁶ in all your ways submit to him, and he will make your paths straight.
⁷ Do not be wise in your own eyes; fear the Lord and shun evil.
⁸ This will bring health to your body and nourishment to your bones.

⁹ Honor the Lord with your wealth, with the firstfruits of all your crops;
¹⁰ then your barns will be filled to overflowing, and your vats will brim over with new wine.

Therefore, trust in God wholeheartedly. Honour Him with your firstfruits. It will be well with your body and soul, as you rely on His wisdom and principles as opposed to our own. While honouring Him with your firstfruits, you will experience the abundant life Jesus promised. "The thief comes only to steal and kill and destroy; I have come that they may have life and have it to the full." (John 10:10)

Prioritising Jesus, by offering our firstfruits and firstborn, is making a statement that God comes first in our life. From experience, I can tell you that when you put God first, expect Him to put you first. There is no discrimination here, for God is not a God of favouritism. However, He is a God of favour. To put it bluntly, we reap what we sow. When you put God first in your life, naturally, His favour rests on you. Giving your firstfruits is basically recognising the Priority of Jesus.

CHAPTER 5

MEMORIAL - RECOGNISING THE COVENANT OF JESUS

A memorial is a rare combination of a promise, attached to a vow, that is made between God and a believer, or, a believer and God. In the case of a believer making a memorial with God, it could involve seeking a breakthrough to an impossible situation. This should not be confused with trying to 'bribe' God or 'bend His Arm', as our God is not a God of favouritism. He chooses to bestow favour on whom He so decides as Sovereign God. In the case of God making a memorial with mankind, it is due to His unfailing love as a reminder to us.

Fasting, for instance, is a great practice to humble oneself before God, and obtain mercy from Him. However, one must not mistake fasting as trying to get special favours from God. It is an act of humbling oneself before Him. (Isaiah 58) When it comes to memorials, we can see in Scripture, where men and women made vows that must be fulfilled, if their requests were granted. This specific kind of offering is known as making a memorial with God.

Genesis 9:12-17
[12] And God said, "This is the sign of the covenant I am making between me and you and every living creature with you, a covenant for all generations to come:
[13] I have set my rainbow in the clouds, and it will be the sign of the covenant between me and the earth.
[14] Whenever I bring clouds over the earth and the rainbow appears in the clouds,
[15] I will remember my covenant between me and you and all living creatures of every kind. Never again will the waters become a flood to destroy all life.
[16] Whenever the rainbow appears in the clouds, I will see it

and remember the everlasting covenant between God and all
living creatures of every kind on the earth."
[17] So God said to Noah, "This is the sign of the covenant I
have established between me and all life on the earth."

The very first time we see God making a memorial with mankind, is after the flood of Noah's time. After the ark rested on
Mount Ararat, Noah offered a freewill offering to God, in commemoration of divine protection from the global catastrophe.
God was pleased with the offering and made an unconditional
covenant with all mankind. He will never destroy the earth by
flood again. Then God made a memorial, in the form of a rainbow, to "remember" His covenant, or more so, as a reminder
to us. We must note that the rainbow was not a sign of God's
'forgetfulness'! It was a memorial, a covenant, a "sign" that
He will keep his promise.

Leviticus 2:1-3
[1] "'When anyone brings a grain offering to the Lord, their
offering is to be of the finest flour. They are to pour olive oil
on it, put incense on it
[2] and take it to Aaron's sons the priests. The priest shall take a
handful of the flour and oil, together with all the incense, and
burn this as a memorial portion on the altar, a food offering,
an aroma pleasing to the Lord.
[3] The rest of the grain offering belongs to Aaron and his sons;
it is a most holy part of the food offerings presented to the
Lord.

The memorial offering was part of the grain offering brought
to God voluntarily, as a devotion. This was not an offering to
pay for sins but an expression of worship, praise, devotion and
thanksgiving. That was what Noah did. (Genesis 8:20-22) It
was not consumed by the person offering it but burned as a
memorial to God. The worshipper did this in honour, reverence and respect for God, knowing God sees the heart. God

receives this freewill gift and will ultimately bless the worshipper in answer to prayers.

While Joshua fought against the five Amorite Kings, he declared (a vow) to destroy the enemies if the sun and moon stayed in position. God not only granted him this seemingly impossible request but was also involved in the destruction of the enemies with hailstones hurled at the fleeing army. This is indeed an impossible situation, but the request came as a memorial to God and he granted Joshua his impossible request.

"On the day the Lord gave the Amorites over to Israel, Joshua said to the Lord in the presence of Israel: "Sun, stand still over Gibeon, and you, moon, over the Valley of Aijalon." So the sun stood still, and the moon stopped, till the nation avenged itself on its enemies, as it is written in the Book of Jashar." (Joshua 10:12-13) The request was humanly impossible, but God allowed it, as it surely was a test to Joshua's vow.

1 Samuel 1:1-20
¹ There was a certain man from Ramathaim, a Zuphite from the hill country of Ephraim, whose name was Elkanah son of Jeroham, the son of Elihu, the son of Tohu, the son of Zuph, an Ephraimite.
² He had two wives; one was called Hannah and the other Peninnah. Peninnah had children, but Hannah had none.
³ Year after year this man went up from his town to worship and sacrifice to the Lord Almighty at Shiloh, where Hophni and Phinehas, the two sons of Eli, were priests of the Lord.
⁴ Whenever the day came for Elkanah to sacrifice, he would give portions of the meat to his wife Peninnah and to all her sons and daughters.
⁵ But to Hannah he gave a double portion because he loved her, and the Lord had closed her womb.
⁶ Because the Lord had closed Hannah's womb, her rival kept provoking her in order to irritate her. ⁷ This went on year af-

ter year. Whenever Hannah went up to the house of the Lord, her rival provoked her till she wept and would not eat.

⁸ Her husband Elkanah would say to her, "Hannah, why are you weeping? Why don't you eat? Why are you downhearted? Don't I mean more to you than ten sons?"

⁹ Once when they had finished eating and drinking in Shiloh, Hannah stood up. Now Eli the priest was sitting on his chair by the doorpost of the Lord's house.

¹⁰ In her deep anguish Hannah prayed to the Lord, weeping bitterly.

¹¹ And she made a vow, saying, "Lord Almighty, if you will only look on your servant's misery and remember me, and not forget your servant but give her a son, then I will give him to the Lord for all the days of his life, and no razor will ever be used on his head."

¹² As she kept on praying to the Lord, Eli observed her mouth.

¹³ Hannah was praying in her heart, and her lips were moving but her voice was not heard. Eli thought she was drunk

¹⁴ and said to her, "How long are you going to stay drunk? Put away your wine."

¹⁵ "Not so, my lord," Hannah replied, "I am a woman who is deeply troubled. I have not been drinking wine or beer; I was pouring out my soul to the Lord.

¹⁶ Do not take your servant for a wicked woman; I have been praying here out of my great anguish and grief."

¹⁷ Eli answered, "Go in peace, and may the God of Israel grant you what you have asked of him."

¹⁸ She said, "May your servant find favor in your eyes." Then she went her way and ate something, and her face was no longer downcast.

¹⁹ Early the next morning they arose and worshiped before the Lord and then went back to their home at Ramah. Elkanah made love to his wife Hannah, and the Lord remembered her.

²⁰ So in the course of time Hannah became pregnant and gave birth to a son. She named him Samuel, saying, "Because I asked the Lord for him."

The story above is about Hannah, who had an impossible situation, in which her rival was constantly tormenting her. In spite of having her husband's favour, her womb was closed, and only God could open it. Understanding the impossibility of her situation, and unable to bear the mockery of her rivals anymore, she appealed to Almighty God in anguish of her soul, with a prayerful vow. In verse 11 we read, "And she made a vow, saying, "Lord Almighty, if you will only look on your servant's misery and remember me, and not forget your servant but give her a son, then I will give him to the Lord for all the days of his life, and no razor will ever be used on his head."

She vowed, recognising God's Sovereignty, and asked Him to look at her misery and made a memorial. "Remember me Lord" – she prayed. A rare prayer mingled with a vow, as a memorial, and in this case, an appeal specifically for a first-born son. Amazingly, her vow for a son was to simply to return him back to God. What an inspiring prayer! The situations and circumstances in her life, brought her to a point where she pleaded with God in agony of soul, and it came up to Him as a memorial. The Lord indeed answered her prayer, and she fulfilled her vow. We read on about Samuel, Hannah's first-born, now ministering before the Lord.

1 Samuel 2:18-21
[18] But Samuel was ministering before the Lord - a boy wearing a linen ephod.
[19] Each year his mother made him a little robe and took it to him when she went up with her husband to offer the annual sacrifice.
[20] Eli would bless Elkanah and his wife, saying, "May the Lord give you children by this woman to take the place of the one she prayed for and gave to the Lord." Then they would go home.
[21] And the Lord was gracious to Hannah; she gave birth to three sons and two daughters. Meanwhile, the boy Samuel

grew up in the presence of the Lord.

This memorial came up before God, and He remembered Hannah. He not only gave her a son, but three more boys and two daughters! She was blessed beyond her request. Samuel went on to be one of the greatest prophets of Israel. This is also due to the heritage of a praying mother, who fulfilled a memorial vow to God, and a devotional and worshipful father, who annually went up to the temple, to offer sacrifices. Her impossible situation came up before God in remembrance, as she made a memorial before Him.

Mark 14:3-9
[3] While he was in Bethany, reclining at the table in the home of Simon the Leper, a woman came with an alabaster jar of very expensive perfume, made of pure nard. She broke the jar and poured the perfume on his head.
[4] Some of those present were saying indignantly to one another, "Why this waste of perfume?
[5] It could have been sold for more than a year's wages and the money given to the poor." And they rebuked her harshly.
[6] "Leave her alone," said Jesus. "Why are you bothering her? She has done a beautiful thing to me. [7] The poor you will always have with you, and you can help them any time you want. But you will not always have me.
[8] She did what she could. She poured perfume on my body beforehand to prepare for my burial. [9] Truly I tell you, wherever the gospel is preached throughout the world, what she has done will also be told, in memory of her."

This passage speaks of a woman who came with a very expensive jar of perfume, worth a year's wages, and poured it on Jesus' head. Whatever the prayer or vow that was in her heart, Jesus not only perceived it, but received the offering and said, she did a "beautiful thing". Unknown to her, she was involved in an epic, eternal and historic event, the preparation Jesus' burial. This offering came up as a memorial, and we still speak of it in memory of her, as Jesus prophesied.

The disciples rebuked her harshly for this lavish gift. Judas left after this incident, to betray Jesus. It is noteworthy to mention here, that our memorial gift to Jesus, can at times be sorely misunderstood by others – especially by His opponents. The point is, this is something between a believer and God. God sees what is in our hearts and knows our thoughts. He is faithful. He never fails.

1 Corinthians 11:23-26
23 For I received from the Lord what I also passed on to you:
The Lord Jesus, on the night he was betrayed, took bread,
24 and when he had given thanks, he broke it and said, "This
is my body, which is for you; do this in remembrance of me."
25 In the same way, after supper he took the cup, saying, "This
cup is the new covenant in my blood; do this, whenever you
drink it, in remembrance of me."
26 For whenever you eat this bread and drink this cup, you
proclaim the Lord's death until he comes.

Perhaps one of the most understated passages in Scriptures concerning a memorial, is the New Covenant, made by Jesus with all believers. Paul clearly states that Jesus wanted the elements of the communion, the bread and the cup, to be partaken in memory of Him. Jesus is making a memorial with all believers, just as God did with mankind after the flood in Noah's time. It is thus appropriate for believers who partake of the Holy Communion, not only to remember the death, burial, resurrection and soon coming of the Lord Jesus, but also to commemorate the New Covenant of love, grace, mercy, forgiveness, repentance, providence, protection and our new transformed life of signs, wonders and miracles.

Acts 10:1-7

¹ At Caesarea there was a man named Cornelius, a centurion in what was known as the Italian Regiment.
² He and all his family were devout and God-fearing; he gave generously to those in need and prayed to God regularly.
³ One day at about three in the afternoon he had a vision. He distinctly saw an angel of God, who came to him and said, "Cornelius!"
⁴ Cornelius stared at him in fear. "What is it, Lord?" he asked.
The angel answered, "Your prayers and gifts to the poor have come up as a memorial offering before God.
⁵ Now send men to Joppa to bring back a man named Simon who is called Peter.
⁶ He is staying with Simon the tanner, whose house is by the sea."
⁷ When the angel who spoke to him had gone, Cornelius called two of his servants and a devout soldier who was one of his attendants.
⁸ He told them everything that had happened and sent them to Joppa.

Cornelius was a God-fearing man who was characterised by his giving to those in need, while being prayerful. Notice, he gave to the needy, not the greedy. Incidentally, some of the most God-fearing people are usually the most generous people too. Proverbs 22:9 says "The generous will themselves be blessed, for they share their food with the poor." As we read above, Cornelius was indeed blessed, as the angel declared to him, in a vision, "Your prayers and gifts to the poor have come up as a memorial offering before God." Cornelius' prayers and gifts made him become the first gentile to whom Peter was commissioned to preach the Gospel, following the outpouring of the Holy Spirit on the day of Pentecost.

The combination of prayers and gifts somehow moves heaven and earth, reaches out to impossible situations, and receives unprecedented favour from God. Among all the gentiles on earth, Cornelius was chosen by God. Peter got very specific instructions from God, to go and preach to this particular and specific gentile. What an honour and favour for Cornelius.

Until then, in spite of our Lord commanding the disciples to preach the gospel to all nations, it was still predominantly a 'Jewish' affair. It was Paul, who later became the apostle to the Gentiles, and went on to preach beyond Israel, thanks to Cornelius' memorial. His prayers and gifts opened the seemingly 'impossible' ministry door to the Gentile world.

Ecclesiastes 5:4-6
⁴ When you make a vow to God, do not delay to fulfill it. He has no pleasure in fools; fulfill your vow.
⁵ It is better not to make a vow than to make one and not fulfill it.
⁶ Do not let your mouth lead you into sin. And do not protest to the temple messenger, "My vow was a mistake." Why should God be angry at what you say and destroy the work of your hands?

As we read from the examples of memorials, it is vital to note that we should not make a vow light heartedly. The warnings from Ecclesiastes states, it is better not to make a vow, rather than to make one and not fulfil it. A memorial is not something we do every day, but as and when we face situations or circumstances that seems impossible. We can invite God into the scenario by making a memorial with Him. This is solely between a believer and God.

Perhaps, a stronghold in your life you need to break. Maybe, it is an impossible relationship that needs mending. Perhaps, you are in a place in life where you have prayed, fasted and tried everything needed, with no results yet. Remember here, that God's answer to your prayers may be 'yes', 'no', 'wait' or

He simply remains silent. God hears all prayers, from sincere hearts, with pure motives. (James 4:3) He still decides the answers as He is Sovereign.

Perhaps, you might develop a conviction in your spirit that your breakthrough, is but a memorial away. If so, go ahead and make a memorial with God. Remember, when your prayer is fulfilled, do not neglect your vow. As we read earlier, "He has no pleasure in fools." (Ecclesiastes 5:4)

When Jesus was present on earth, he had a single goal, as stated in His own words - "to do the will of him who sent me and to finish his work". (John 4:34) That will, was to make the Father and Son known to us. (John 17:3) This work was completed on the cross, when he said, "It is finished". (John 21:30) This offering on the cross is symbolic of an eternal memorial, as this Lamb was slain from the foundations of the earth. (Revelations 13:8b)

Jesus was, and is, that Eternal Lamb that was covenanted for us. The determination of Jesus to endure the cross, scorning its shame, and to sit down at the right hand of the Father, making intercession for us till today, should be enough hope and encouragement for all believers to take our impossible situations to God in a memorial. (Hebrews 12:1-3) Our Lord, our God, our Friend and our Brother, Jesus Christ, is still praying for us today.

Besides, Jesus did not leave us alone - he left us with the Holy Spirit, to be our comforter until we meet Him again. (John 16:7) The Holy Spirit will guide you to all truth. When led by the Holy Spirit to make a memorial with God, go ahead and have your breakthrough. (John 16:13) Making a memorial is basically recognising the Covenant of Jesus.

CHAPTER 6

SOWING AND REAPING – RECOGNISING THE REWARDS OF JESUS

The principle of sowing and reaping is yet another aspect of Biblical Economy. Here, believers are encouraged to be specific with their sowing, expecting a harvest, in order to repeat the process. As mentioned earlier, God wants us to be blessed, so that we can be a blessing, as stated to Abraham. (Genesis 12:1-3) The concept of sowing and reaping is an agricultural principle, and God uses this to imply that while we sow diligently, we will reap a harvest of abundance. Again, this reaping is not for selfish or self-centred purposes, but to be an extension of God's Arm of Blessings.

Genesis 8:20-22
20 Then Noah built an altar to the Lord and, taking some of all the clean animals and clean birds, he sacrificed burnt offerings on it.
21 The Lord smelled the pleasing aroma and said in his heart:
"Never again will I curse the ground because of humans,
even though every inclination of the human heart is evil from childhood. And never again will I destroy all living creatures, as I have done.
22 "As long as the earth endures, seedtime and harvest,
cold and heat, summer and winter, day and night will never cease."

After the flood and destruction of the wicked and sinful generation during the time of Noah, perpetrated by Adam and Eve's sin, and exploited by the fallen angels, Noah exits the ark and offers freewill offerings to the Lord. God smells the aroma and is pleased in His heart. Then God makes an unconditional covenant with Noah, not to destroy the earth by flood again, and pronounces some everlasting principles that exist to date. Among them was seedtime and harvest, or in other words, sowing and reaping.

This principle is beyond agricultural, and affects economy too, as we will explore further, and the very moral principles of mankind. Paul states in Galatians 6:7-10, "Do not be deceived: God cannot be mocked. A man reaps what he sows. Whoever sows to please their flesh, from the flesh will reap destruction; whoever sows to please the Spirit, from the Spirit will reap eternal life. Let us not become weary in doing good, for at the proper time we will reap a harvest if we do not give up. Therefore, as we have opportunity, let us do good to all people, especially to those who belong to the family of believers."

Life in general, according to Scriptures, is a reaping of what one sows. Sowing to the carnal nature will reap destruction. Sowing to the Spirit will reap eternal life. Thus, we are encouraged to pursue godliness, as it will produce a harvest of righteousness in our life. We are also encouraged not to give up, and remain consistent, as sowing can become tedious and tiring. Yet, the one who sows conscientiously and constantly in life, will have a never-ending stream of harvest, and seeds left over.

Back to economy, the purpose of sowing and reaping is not to give to the poor as in alms, nor make a memorial with God for an impossible situation. Instead, this principle is solely rooted in seeking the right kind of 'soil' to sow into, while expecting a return. Again, this is not a 'selfish', act but rather a deliberate act of diligent investment.

For instance, when one invests in the stock market, one will diligently follow the performance of the stocks, in order to predict a yield from the investment. Likewise, sowing and reaping is to look for opportunities to invest into the Kingdom of God, in order to receive blessings from God to repeat the process.

Not every believer may have this mindset. There are those who understand and practice it. "Remember this: Whoever sows sparingly will also reap sparingly, and whoever sows generously will also reap generously." (2 Corinthians 9:6) Thus, "whoever" refers to those who understand and practice. Not all believers do.

Jesus Himself explained the principle of sowing and reaping, in relation to the Word of God being sown. We read about this principle in Matthew 13, when he first spoke in parables and later explained the parable to His disciples. Notice, the principle of sowing and reaping in play.

Matthew 13:3-9
³ Then he told them many things in parables, saying: "A farmer went out to sow his seed.
⁴ As he was scattering the seed, some fell along the path, and the birds came and ate it up.
⁵ Some fell on rocky places, where it did not have much soil. It sprang up quickly, because the soil was shallow.
⁶ But when the sun came up, the plants were scorched, and they withered because they had no root.
⁷ Other seed fell among thorns, which grew up and choked the plants.
⁸ Still other seed fell on good soil, where it produced a crop - a hundred, sixty or thirty times what was sown.
⁹ Whoever has ears, let them hear."

After sharing the parable to the public, Jesus privately explains the meaning of it to his disciples.

Matthew 13:18-23
¹⁸ "Listen then to what the parable of the sower means:
¹⁹ When anyone hears the message about the kingdom and does not understand it, the evil one comes and snatches away what was sown in their heart. This is the seed sown along the

path.

20 The seed falling on rocky ground refers to someone who hears the word and at once receives it with joy.

21 But since they have no root, they last only a short time. When trouble or persecution comes because of the word, they quickly fall away.

22 The seed falling among the thorns refers to someone who hears the word, but the worries of this life and the deceitfulness of wealth choke the word, making it unfruitful.

23 But the seed falling on good soil refers to someone who hears the word and understands it. This is the one who produces a crop, yielding a hundred, sixty or thirty times what was sown."

Though the context of the passage is in regard to the message about the Kingdom of God, the principle of sowing and reaping is explained. Sowing in the wrong places will not yield results. Instead, sowing in good soil will reap a harvest of hundredfold, sixtyfold or thirtyfold results. If we look at this from an economical perspective, I do not know of any bank on earth that will give you such returns for your investment. However, the 'Bank of Heaven' does! When we invest in good soil, as in a church, ministry or a person whom God may lay on your heart, expect a bountiful harvest from God.

In every church I have led, I encouraged the congregation to sow into missions, missionaries or churches who are doing well. We not only have helped those struggling with finances (as in alms), we also deliberately give to those who are doing a good job (as in sowing), so they can do even better. One aspect of missions is alms, and the other is sowing and reaping. As a result, God has always provided funds to us, in order to remain a blessing. This is a divine principle. Therefore, Paul encouraged the Corinthians to follow the example of the Macedonians, who were known for their extravagant giving.

2 Corinthians 9:6-15

⁶ Remember this: Whoever sows sparingly will also reap sparingly, and whoever sows generously will also reap generously.

⁷ Each of you should give what you have decided in your heart to give, not reluctantly or under compulsion, for God loves a cheerful giver.

⁸ And God is able to bless you abundantly, so that in all things at all times, having all that you need, you will abound in every good work.

⁹ As it is written: "They have freely scattered their gifts to the poor; their righteousness endures forever."

¹⁰ Now he who supplies seed to the sower and bread for food will also supply and increase your store of seed and will enlarge the harvest of your righteousness.

¹¹ You will be enriched in every way so that you can be generous on every occasion, and through us your generosity will result in thanksgiving to God.

¹² This service that you perform is not only supplying the needs of the Lord's people but is also overflowing in many expressions of thanks to God.

¹³ Because of the service by which you have proved yourselves, others will praise God for the obedience that accompanies your confession of the gospel of Christ, and for your generosity in sharing with them and with everyone else.

¹⁴ And in their prayers for you their hearts will go out to you, because of the surpassing grace God has given you.

¹⁵ Thanks be to God for his indescribable gift!

The principle Paul uses to illustrate their gift was that of sowing and reaping. Believers were encouraged to sow generously and not sparingly. This should be done cheerfully, and with a willing heart. Not grudgingly, as God loves a cheerful giver, as He is a Cheerful Giver. Moreover, having all your needs amply met, God will bless you at all times, to remain a continual blessing. The bonus of being a sower is that, your seed store will be enlarged, to produce a harvest of righteousness.

In the meantime, you will be enriched in every way, in order to be generous, and your gifts will produce thanksgiving to God. In the preceding chapter, Paul explained the attitude of the Macedonians who excelled in the grace of giving, and wanted the Corinthians to excel in that gift as well. As I write this book, my hopes and prayers are that every believer excels in the grace of giving, or at least, be inspired to do so, after understanding all 7 Biblical Economic Principles.

2 Corinthians 8:1-15
[1] And now, brothers and sisters, we want you to know about the grace that God has given the Macedonian churches.
[2] In the midst of a very severe trial, their overflowing joy and their extreme poverty welled up in rich generosity.
[3] For I testify that they gave as much as they were able, and even beyond their ability. Entirely on their own,
[4] they urgently pleaded with us for the privilege of sharing in this service to the Lord's people.
[5] And they exceeded our expectations: They gave themselves first of all to the Lord, and then by the will of God also to us.
[6] So we urged Titus, just as he had earlier made a beginning, to bring also to completion this act of grace on your part.
[7] But since you excel in everything - in faith, in speech, in knowledge, in complete earnestness and in the love we have kindled in you - see that you also excel in this grace of giving.
[8] I am not commanding you, but I want to test the sincerity of your love by comparing it with the earnestness of others.
[9] For you know the grace of our Lord Jesus Christ, that though he was rich, yet for your sake he became poor, so that you through his poverty might become rich.
[10] And here is my judgment about what is best for you in this matter. Last year you were the first not only to give but also to have the desire to do so.
[11] Now finish the work, so that your eager willingness to do it

may be matched by your completion of it, according to your means.

[12] For if the willingness is there, the gift is acceptable according to what one has, not according to what one does not have.
[13] Our desire is not that others might be relieved while you are hard pressed, but that there might be equality.
[14] At the present time your plenty will supply what they need, so that in turn their plenty will supply what you need. The goal is equality,
[15] as it is written: "The one who gathered much did not have too much, and the one who gathered little did not have too little."

The Macedonians had a special grace of giving. We should all pray and ask God for this grace. When they gave, they were not rich, but in fact, were in extreme poverty. Holding back from giving with poverty as an excuse is not Biblical - it is simply an excuse. Out of their "extreme poverty", the Macedonians welled up in rich generosity. We do not have to be rich, in order to sow-- just willing. This happened because they first gave themselves up to the Lord. When you give up, you will be able to give all - nothing will hold you back.

For those struggling in the grace of giving, perhaps you should first give yourself up to the Lord in complete surrender. This will help you understand that everything you have is indeed from Him, and He will never leave you nor forsake you, let alone leave you empty handed. Psalm 37:25 says, "I was young and now I am old, yet I have never seen the righteous forsaken or their children begging bread." The grace of giving is a divine gift from heaven, which all believers should aspire to have and grow into, in spite of our economic status. Start by surrendering to the Lord unconditionally.

Notice, giving oneself up to the Lord speaks of a devotional intimate relationship with Jesus Christ. We must constantly re-examine our relationship with Jesus. We cannot 'give out' if we have not 'given up'. Give up your selfish ambitions and vain conceits and submit totally without holding back from God. Philippians 2:3-4, says, "Do nothing out of selfish ambition or vain conceit. Rather, in humility value others above yourselves, not looking to your own interests but each of you to the interests of the others." In that light, your perspective of who He is and who we are, including all we have, will get into the right perspective. An old song states, "Turn your eyes upon Jesus, look full in His wonderful grace. And the things of the earth will grow strangely dim. In the light, of His glory and grace."

The Macedonians were following the example Jesus set for us. Jesus became poor, so that through Him, we might become rich. 2 Corinthians 8:9 says, "For you know the grace of our Lord Jesus Christ, that though he was rich, yet for your sake he became poor, so that you through his poverty might become rich." Each follower of Christ should reflect the nature of Christ, being a giver, not a grabber. Sowing into others, not seeking rewards.

In sowing and reaping, ask God to lead you to the right person, ministry, church, organisation or any other fertile soil. When sowing, it is with a specific intention to expect a harvest from God. Your intension must be to sow, God's part is to reward you of your investment. With the reward reaped, you may continue the process all over again. In reality, this is divine partnership with God.

Sowing is to seek those doing a good job, and help them make it great. Over the years, personally and in ministry, I have done this. This is not done to meet a need or a crisis, rather, it is intentional because of the principle of sowing and reaping. We know that as we sow, we will reap. To the Glory of God, to date, God has continuously kept my 'seed bank' full. It is always a joy and honour to serve with God.

Among others, we also seek how to be a blessing to Israel, as God told Abraham that "I will bless those who bless you, and whoever curses you I will curse." (Genesis 12:3) Thus, the church I lead, financially contributes to a Messianic Jewish Congregation, that God led us to support. We do this in obedience of a Biblical Principle and thank God for His faithfulness to us.

We also conduct biannual Educational Tours to Israel, to educate saints about the land and its Biblical history, while blessing the economy of the nation with tourism. These kinds of sowing naturally pleases God, and we are still reaping the benefits of it. "Let us not become weary in doing good, for at the proper time we will reap a harvest if we do not give up." (Galatians 6:9)

It is my belief that God is looking for vessels on earth, through whom He can be a channel of blessings to multitudes. Such vessels should be seen to be faithful in tithing, offerings, alms, firstfruits, and memorials before becoming a candidate of sowing and reaping. Perhaps you are a candidate to be God's Financier on this planet, in these last days. Isaiah 45:3 says, "I will give you hidden treasures, riches stored in secret places, so that you may know that I am the Lord, the God of Israel, who summons you by name." Excel in Biblical economic principles and experience God's abundant storehouse, which has unlimited capacity, and no economic crisis. Sowing and reaping is basically recognising the Rewards of Jesus.

CHAPTER 7

SACRIFICIAL GIVING – RECOGNISING THE ULTIMATE LOVE OF JESUS

Sacrificial giving is perhaps the epitome and ultimate of all giving. This is a gift that costs the giver dearly. It is not giving out of abundance. It is literally giving up, what may rightfully belong to you. God demonstrated this by giving up His one and only Son. Jesus laid down His life for us. He did not have to, but He did it, because of love. Sacrificial giving should never be taken lightly, as there is a high price to pay for it, albeit, for divine love.

Genesis 3:21
²¹ The Lord God made garments of skin for Adam and his wife and clothed them.

An important verse, that could be easily overlooked, with regards to the fall of mankind in Genesis 3, is verse 21. Something happened here - God made garments of skin to cover their nakedness. An innocent animal had to be sacrificed, in what was a perfect world, before sin. This was the first bloodshed on planet earth. The first life that was sacrificed. The animal had to give all, in order to cover the shame and nakedness of mankind.

This was a foreshadow of the Lamb of God, who will give all, in order to redeem the sins of all mankind - the ultimate sacrifice. A sin he did not deserve. He was not the cause of it, yet, because of love, he paid the ultimate price. In that light, when we read yet another famous passage in the Bible, we can quickly read past three very important words in John 3:16.

John 3:16-21
¹⁶ For God so loved the world that he gave his one and only

Son, that whoever believes in him shall not perish but have eternal life.
¹⁷ For God did not send his Son into the world to condemn the world, but to save the world through him.
¹⁸ Whoever believes in him is not condemned, but whoever does not believe stands condemned already because they have not believed in the name of God's one and only Son.
¹⁹ This is the verdict: Light has come into the world, but people loved darkness instead of light because their deeds were evil.
²⁰ Everyone who does evil hates the light, and will not come into the light for fear that their deeds will be exposed.
²¹ But whoever lives by the truth comes into the light, so that it may be seen plainly that what they have done has been done in the sight of God.

Notice it says in verse 16, "one and only". When God gave Jesus to the world, it was His ultimate act of giving - Sacrificial Giving. God was not sparing one of his many sons. There was only ONE! It was the Ultimate Sacrifice. The ultimate expression of love. He gave up the best - nothing less. It was this sacrificial giving that purchased our salvation. This salvation is free, but not at all cheap, by any means.

Therefore, when we share the gospel with unbelievers, it is vital to point out the cost of it, purchased with love. It is for this reason that every believer should never take their salvation for granted. This is why we adore and worship God in awe, wonder, respect, reverence and humility. We owed a debt we could not pay. He paid a 'debt' He did not owe. Amazing grace!

1 Chronicles 21:22-26
²² David said to him, "Let me have the site of your threshing floor so I can build an altar to the Lord, that the plague on the people may be stopped. Sell it to me at the full price."
²³ Araunah said to David, "Take it! Let my lord the king do

whatever pleases him. Look, I will give the oxen for the burnt offerings, the threshing sledges for the wood, and the wheat for the grain offering. I will give all this."

24 But King David replied to Araunah, "No, I insist on paying the full price. I will not take for the Lord what is yours, or sacrifice a burnt offering that costs me nothing."

25 So David paid Araunah six hundred shekels of gold for the site.

26 David built an altar to the Lord there and sacrificed burnt offerings and fellowship offerings. He called on the Lord, and the Lord answered him with fire from heaven on the altar of burnt offering.

When Satan incited David to count the fighting men, in 1 Chronicles 21, David sinned against God and against Joab's advice, bringing guilt on Israel. As a result, Gad was sent by God to David to decide among three judgments God was about to carry out. David choose to fall into the hand of the Lord, and a plague was sent that destroyed seventy thousand men. Then God relented, and David saw the angel of God with a drawn sword between heaven and earth. David repented in sackcloth and ashes. Then God sent Gad to tell David to build an altar, over the place the angel stood, the threshing floor and Araunah.

David wanted to buy that threshing floor at a cost, as he realized the gravity of his sin against God, and the nation of Israel. He said in verse 24, "No, I insist on paying the full price. I will not take for the Lord what is yours or sacrifice a burnt offering that costs me nothing." This is a sacrificial offering. It cost David seventy thousand men and the price of the threshing floor. This real estate would later become the ground on which King Solomon would build the Temple. David learned about sacrifice, the very hard way, as it cost him greatly, along with the loss of many innocent lives.

Later in his Kingdom, David wanted to build a temple, or a

dwelling place for God, which project was assigned to Solomon by God. However, in 1 Chronicles 22:14-16 we read the pains David went through to provide for this project. "I have taken great pains to provide for the temple of the Lord a hundred thousand talents of gold, a million talents of silver, quantities of bronze and iron too great to be weighed, and wood and stone. And you may add to them. You have many workers: stonecutters, masons and carpenters, as well as those skilled in every kind of work in gold and silver, bronze and iron - craftsmen beyond number. Now begin the work, and the Lord be with you." This was a sacrificial offering from David. He surely remembered the cost to stop the plague, but now, he was expressing his devotion, in careful sacrificial offering for the house of God.

1 Chronicles 29:1-5
¹ Then King David said to the whole assembly: "My son Solomon, the one whom God has chosen, is young and inexperienced. The task is great, because this palatial structure is not for man but for the Lord God.
² With all my resources I have provided for the temple of my God - gold for the gold work, silver for the silver, bronze for the bronze, iron for the iron and wood for the wood, as well as onyx for the settings, turquoise, stones of various colors, and all kinds of fine stone and marble - all of these in large quantities.
³ Besides, in my devotion to the temple of my God I now give my personal treasures of gold and silver for the temple of my God, over and above everything I have provided for this holy temple: ⁴ three thousand talents of gold (gold of Ophir) and seven thousand talents of refined silver, for the overlaying of the walls of the buildings,
⁵ for the gold work and the silver work, and for all the work to be done by the craftsmen. Now, who is willing to consecrate themselves to the Lord today?"

David not only gave out of the national treasury, but went out of his way to give from his personal treasury as well, as we read in verses 3-5. This sacrificial gift inspired the leaders and commanders to follow suit. One is often inspired by the sacrificial giving of another. David did this because of his devotion to God, and he was a man after God's own heart. This kind of sacrificial giving does not happen every day, but when the occasion presented itself, David went beyond the line of duty, due to his devotion to God.

In relation to that, another form of sacrificial giving for believers, is the daily denial of our sinful nature, in order to follow Christ. Today, our bodies are the Temple of God in which He dwells. Each time we say 'no' to sin and 'yes' to righteousness, it is a form of taking up our cross and denying our sinful nature. That too, is a sacrificial offering - an aroma pleasing to God. Because God sacrificed His Son on the Cross, we are inspired to respond in love, sacrificially, and, to symbolically take up our cross daily and follow Him.

1 Kings 17:7-16
[7] Some time later the brook dried up because there had been no rain in the land.
[8] Then the word of the Lord came to him:
[9] "Go at once to Zarephath in the region of Sidon and stay there. I have directed a widow there to supply you with food."
[10] So he went to Zarephath. When he came to the town gate, a widow was there gathering sticks. He called to her and asked, "Would you bring me a little water in a jar so I may have a drink?"
[11] As she was going to get it, he called, "And bring me, please, a piece of bread."
[12] "As surely as the Lord your God lives," she replied, "I don't have any bread - only a handful of flour in a jar and a little olive oil in a jug. I am gathering a few sticks to take home and make a meal for myself and my son, that we may

eat it - and die."

13 Elijah said to her, "Don't be afraid. Go home and do as you have said. But first make a small loaf of bread for me from what you have and bring it to me, and then make something for yourself and your son.

14 For this is what the Lord, the God of Israel, says: 'The jar of flour will not be used up and the jug of oil will not run dry until the day the Lord sends rain on the land.'"

15 She went away and did as Elijah had told her. So there was food every day for Elijah and for the woman and her family.

16 For the jar of flour was not used up and the jug of oil did not run dry, in keeping with the word of the Lord spoken by Elijah.

The story of Elijah and the widow at Zarephath is yet another example of a sacrificial gift that brought the widow and her son supernatural supply, in a time of drought in the land. Elijah knew the bleak condition of her poverty and the severe drought in the land. Yet, as inspired by God, he told the widow to first, bring him a loaf of bread. One can say the principle of the 'first', as in firstfruits, and the principle of sacrificial offering, were in operation here. It must have taken much faith for the widow to do what Elijah asked, but she did it, and God honoured her faith.

Because the widow sacrificed by faith, through the words of the man of God, the jar of flour was not used up and the jug of oil did not run dry. Sacrificial giving can usher us into God's supernatural providence, in spite of what the climate or global economic conditions are. Biblical economic principles supersede that of the world. When prompted by the Holy Spirit to sacrifice, especially in times of need or want, remember that when we seek God first, He will meet our needs. (Matthew 6:33)

Luke 21:1-4
¹ As Jesus looked up, he saw the rich putting their gifts into the temple treasury.
² He also saw a poor widow put in two very small copper coins.
³ "Truly I tell you," he said, "this poor widow has put in more than all the others.
⁴ All these people gave their gifts out of their wealth; but she out of her poverty put in all she had to live on."

In Luke 21:1-4, we read of yet another widow, in the act of giving a sacrificial offering. Notice, Jesus was observing the offerings. The next time you are in church, and the offering time comes around, remember that Jesus is watching. What caught Jesus' attention was not what the rich gave, out of their abundance, but that this poor widow, who sacrificed all she had. This offering touched Jesus and He said, she gave "more than all the others". It was more than the value of the gift, but the principle of it thereof; it was all she had. It was a sacrificial giving. A sacrificial giving always speaks of Jesus Himself. Jesus became our ultimate sacrifice.

Some use this passage to state, it does not matter how much we give, as long as we give. A proper understanding of the passage will indicate that it was not the amount that was in focus here, it was the principle of sacrifice. It is not a matter of rich or poor, it was a matter of what was left over. Any rich man could have done the same. Once, a rich man was challenged to give sacrificially to Jesus. However, he could not pay the price - he walked away.

Mark 10:17-22
¹⁷ As Jesus started on his way, a man ran up to him and fell on his knees before him. "Good teacher," he asked, "what must I do to inherit eternal life?"
¹⁸ "Why do you call me good?" Jesus answered. "No one is

good - except God alone.
19 You know the commandments: 'You shall not murder, you shall not commit adultery, you shall not steal, you shall not give false testimony, you shall not defraud, honor your father and mother.'"
20 "Teacher," he declared, "all these I have kept since I was a boy."
21 Jesus looked at him and loved him. "One thing you lack," he said. "Go, sell everything you have and give to the poor, and you will have treasure in heaven. Then come, follow me."
22 At this the man's face fell. He went away sad, because he had great wealth.

It is vital to understand here, that this was not a general pre-condition in order to become a disciple of Jesus. We are not told that we should sell everything and give to the poor before we can be a disciple. In this particular case, this man had done everything right. However, something was holding him back - his great wealth. Because it was a stronghold in his life, Jesus loved him, and challenged him to sacrifice all his wealth.

The man could not do it, and simply turned around and walked away. There are many people on earth who do good, even know Jesus, but find it difficult to pay the ultimate price when challenged by Jesus in certain aspects. There may be times in our life, when the Holy Spirit tugs at our conscience to give something up. When this happens, do not hesitate for a moment, and submit to God.

This may not necessarily be wealth. It may be a career, a hobby, an unequally yoked relationship, a habit, or something else that has taken the place of God in our life. Our God is a jealous God and will not share His glory with another; let alone let it take His place. Ironically, as for the rich man, if he had stayed a little longer, instead of walking away, he would have heard what Jesus said later to his disciples. He would have been richly rewarded if he sacrificed.

Mark 10:23-30
23 Jesus looked around and said to his disciples, "How hard it is for the rich to enter the kingdom of God!"
24 The disciples were amazed at his words. But Jesus said again, "Children, how hard it is to enter the kingdom of God! 25 It is easier for a camel to go through the eye of a needle than for someone who is rich to enter the kingdom of God."
26 The disciples were even more amazed, and said to each other, "Who then can be saved?"
27 Jesus looked at them and said, "With man this is impossible, but not with God; all things are possible with God."
28 Then Peter spoke up, "We have left everything to follow you!"
29 "Truly I tell you," Jesus replied, "no one who has left home or brothers or sisters or mother or father or children or fields for me and the gospel
30 will fail to receive a hundred times as much in this present age: homes, brothers, sisters, mothers, children and fields— along with persecutions—and in the age to come eternal life. 31 But many who are first will be last, and the last first."

Jesus taught that it was difficult, but not impossible, for the rich to enter the Kingdom of God. When riches become our security, God becomes a subsidiary. When riches are a subsidiary, God becomes our security. Peter was perplexed by this, as by then, he and the other disciples had sacrificially left everything to follow Christ. It is comforting to hear Jesus' response in verses 29-30. Whatever we have sacrificed for the gospel, it will be returned a hundred times, in this present age, in spite of persecutions, and eternal life in the age to come. We will be blessed greatly if we sacrificially give.

I have wondered much about the persecution aspect of the totality of God's blessings. It could be that when we are so blessed, men may be jealous of our blessings, and that may attract persecution. We must understand that being blessed, does not exclude, but rather, includes persecution. Jesus Himself said, "if they persecuted me, they will persecute you also." (John 15:20)

The promise of Jesus is that, when we sacrificially give, He will bless us both in this age and the age to come. This sacrificial giving can only be born of the Spirit, into our spirit, as we are inspired in a devotional relationship, to give everything up. As giving is a grace, it is also a spiritual act. One may have a spirit of giving, just as one may be influenced by a spirit of poverty. There are many poor people who possess a spirit of sacrificial generosity, while there are many rich people who are hindered by a spirit of poverty. What an irony?

The concept of sacrificial giving goes beyond material and social benefits. In Romans 12:1-2, Paul urges us to become a living sacrifice to God. "Therefore, I urge you, brothers and sisters, in view of God's mercy, to offer your bodies as a living sacrifice, holy and pleasing to God - this is your true and proper worship. Do not conform to the pattern of this world, but be transformed by the renewing of your mind. Then you will be able to test and approve what God's will is - his good, pleasing and perfect will." We do so daily, by not conforming to the pattern, principles or ways of this world, but by renewing our mind with the pattern, principles and ways of God.

Let not the world squeeze you into its mould. Instead, be a living sacrifice, serving and pleasing God. By so doing, you will not only discover the will of God, you will also have a renewed mind. This Mind of Christ will generate the Character of Christ in us. (1 Corinthians 2:16) The will of God is good, perfect and pleasing. The will of the enemy is bad, imperfect and displeasing. Therefore, choose the sacrificial will of God.

In Hebrews 13:15-16, we are urged to bring a sacrifice of praise and generosity. "Through Jesus, therefore, let us continually offer to God a sacrifice of praise - the fruit of lips that openly profess his name. And do not forget to do good and to share with others, for with such sacrifices God is pleased." Again, a sacrifice of praise is when you praise God, not because you feel like it or can 'afford' to do it. A sacrifice of praise comes forth in difficult times, when the last thing your flesh wants to do is to praise God.

In times of difficulty, sickness, disease, death, depression, oppression, economic and social challenges of all kinds, bring Him a sacrifice of praise, and continue to do good by sharing kindness with others. With such sacrifices, God is pleased. Sing to the Lord a new song. Let everything that has breath praise the Lord. (Ephesians 5:19)

In Psalm 50:17-18, we are challenged to sacrifice to God, and call upon him in times of trouble. "Sacrifice thank offerings to God, fulfil your vows to the Most High, and call on me in the day of trouble; I will deliver you, and you will honor me." Our deliverance will make us honour Him.

Notice, the sacrifice is connected to a vow in this case. God himself promises to be our deliverer when we reach out to him with a sacrificial offering of gratitude. It takes faith to offer sacrificial thanks to God. What you are saying in reality is, "God, I do not yet have the answer to my prayers, and indeed cannot see how this crisis is going to be over. However, knowing you can make a way, even when there seems no way, I thank you by faith for the answer and praise Your Name."

After committing sin with Beersheba, David wrote Psalm 51 and in verses 16-17, he declares, "You do not delight in sacrifice, or I would bring it; you do not take pleasure in burnt offerings. My sacrifice, O God, is a broken spirit; a broken and contrite heart you, God, will not despise." As King, David could have offered countless numbers of sacrifices on the altar, yet he realized, the greatest sacrifice was - a broken spirit and a contrite heart. One that would be sensitive to conviction of sin, and the voice of God. A broken heart, after God's own heart. He learned that this was the sacrifice acceptable to God.

Our sacrificial giving should not come only from wealth, or materials things, but out of a sincere heart of love for God. Hebrews 13:5-6 says, "Keep your lives free from the love of money and be content with what you have, because God has said, "Never will I leave you; never will I forsake you." So we say with confidence, "The Lord is my helper; I will not be afraid. What can mere mortals do to me?" When our confidence is in God, and we know our help comes from Him, because we have a devotional relationship with Him, there will be nothing on earth we will not be willing to sacrificially part with. When we have God, we have everything. Without Him, we have nothing. (Matthew 16:28)

Therefore, Mark 16:26 states, "What good will it be for someone to gain the whole world, yet forfeit their soul? Or what can anyone give in exchange for their soul?" The ultimate is not to gain the whole world, it is to gain God. This world promises us the lust of the eyes, the lust of the flesh and pride of life, with all its glitters, glamour, horns and whistles. Jesus invites us to sacrifice and give up at the feet of the Cross. In return, we gain everything, and eternal life with Him forever.

We read, time and again, in the early church, how believers sold their properties and possessions and left all the funds at the feet of the apostles to meet needs. (Acts 2:44-45; 4:32-37; 5:1-10) We also read of ingenuine people, like Ananias and Sapphira, who pretended to be sacrificial, but lied to the Holy Spirit. They reaped the consequences of their actions with death, as we should not mock God, nor make light of the principle of sacrificial giving for fame or fortune.

When we arrive at a place in our walk with God, where we can say like Paul did, "for me to live is Christ and to die is gain" (Philippians 1:21), then we no longer look at sacrifice as lost, but as a gain. Truly, all aspects of giving are nothing less than a mere response of worship to God, for His efforts made to mend our broken relationship with Him. This relationship can only be restored in and through Jesus. You see, it is all about Jesus. Giving without recognizing Jesus is nothing but an empty and void religion.

If we pay our tithes, offer our offerings, give alms, offer first-fruits, make memorials, sow, reap and sacrifice without having a devotional relationship with God, are we not walking in the footsteps of Cain? God does not need our sacrifices or offe-rings; He truly possesses everything. He wants our love and devotion. When we offer gifts to God in recognition of what God has done for us through Christ, we give worshipfully and with a conviction from the Holy Spirit. The next time you en-gage in any of the principles of giving, may God inspire you to let nothing come between you and Him. May our offerings and sacrifices be a pleasing aroma, acceptable to Him. Sacrificial giving is basically recognising the Ultimate Love of Jesus.

CHAPTER 8

BIBLICAL FINANACIAL MANAGEMENT - A CALL TO GOD'S PRINCIPLES

There are many other passages in Scriptures, concerning the 7 Biblical Economic Principles, which I hope and pray that readers will be inspired to study and discover for themselves. This book's primary purpose is to point out that, each principle is Biblical, and that they stand on their own. They have been presented to inspire you to practice them, because of your love and devotion to Jesus, not because we give religiously let alone reluctantly.

Acts 17:24-31
[24] "The God who made the world and everything in it is the Lord of heaven and earth and does not live in temples built by human hands.
[25] And he is not served by human hands, as if he needed anything. Rather, he himself gives everyone life and breath and everything else.
[26] From one man he made all the nations, that they should inhabit the whole earth; and he marked out their appointed times in history and the boundaries of their lands.
[27] God did this so that they would seek him and perhaps reach out for him and find him, though he is not far from any one of us.
[28] 'For in him we live and move and have our being.' As some of your own poets have said, 'We are his offspring.'
[29] "Therefore since we are God's offspring, we should not think that the divine being is like gold or silver or stone - an image made by human design and skill.
[30] In the past God overlooked such ignorance, but now he commands all people everywhere to repent.
[31] For he has set a day when he will judge the world with justice by the man he has appointed. He has given proof of this

to everyone by raising him from the dead."

While in Athens, Paul taught about the greatness and sovereignty of God. Here, he explained that unlike other gods, our God created all things and does not need anything from us. He created us, provided for us, and sustains us, so that we will recognise Him, seek Him, reach out to Him and worship Him. Indeed, in the past, God overlooked ignorance of mankind in worshipping idols. After the coming of Jesus, He now commands us to repent because Jesus will return to judge the world. Therefore, our devotional worship to God matters now, more than ever before.

1. When you pay your tithe, you recognise the Lordship of Jesus.

2. When you offer your offerings, you recognise the work of Jesus, and want to support it.

3. When you give alms, you recognise the kindness of Jesus, and want to be an extension of it.

4. When you bring your firstfruits or redeem your firstborn, you recognise the priority of Jesus.

5. When you make a memorial, you recognise the covenant of Jesus.

6. When you sow in expectation to reap, you recognise the rewards of Jesus.

7. When you sacrificially give, you recognise the ultimate gift of Jesus.

All seven principles are meant to be practiced as a result of the believers' ongoing relationship with Jesus. Without it, we will simply be practising a meaningless religious ritual, as if God needed something from us. God created everything and has need for nothing! The honour and privilege extended to us, is to be able to bring Him something, and that should never be taken for granted.

We do not give to seek rewards. We give because of love and devotion. However, knowing our generous God, He will bless our giving, when we do it wholeheartedly, understanding Scriptural principles. God is not a debtor to any person, and no one can ever out give God.

It is appropriate in closing this book, to look at some Biblical financial principles about management. When God created the Garden of Eden and placed Adam and Eve there, four rivers ran through the garden to water and nourish it.

Genesis 2:10-14
[10] A river watering the garden flowed from Eden; from there it was separated into four headwaters.
[11] The name of the first is the Pishon; it winds through the entire land of Havilah, where there is gold.
[12] (The gold of that land is good; aromatic resin and onyx are also there.)
[13] The name of the second river is the Gihon; it winds through the entire land of Cush.
[14] The name of the third river is the Tigris; it runs along the east side of Ashur. And the fourth river is the Euphrates.

The above passage is vital, as it speaks of the life sources, watering the Garden of Eden. God wanted Adam to have four different sources to rely on, not only one. This symbolically speaks of our possible sources of supply today. It is common for people to rely only on one source of income, throughout their entire lifetime.

However, I challenge you to be creative and look at the talents you have been endowed with. God has knitted us with every skill and talent we will ever need from our mother's womb, even before birth. It is my belief, that if each person seeks God for divine wisdom, He will give you creative ideas to have more than one source of income throughout your life. This will be very helpful, especially if one source 'dries up', you will have other sources to rely on. This takes wisdom, creativity and divine guidance.

We can easily be accustomed to the ways of the world and believe that things will continue as it always has been. However, according to the Bible, a time will come when this world will be shaken to its core, and all worldly systems that mankind trusted and relied on will be shaken. In such a time, we will need to rely on Biblical principles that will not be shaken. Heaven and earth will pass away, but God's Words will remain forever - unshaken.

Haggai 2:6-9
⁶ "This is what the Lord Almighty says: 'In a little while I will once more shake the heavens and the earth, the sea and the dry land.
⁷ I will shake all nations, and what is desired by all nations will come, and I will fill this house with glory,' says the Lord Almighty.
⁸ 'The silver is mine and the gold is mine,' declares the Lord Almighty.
⁹ 'The glory of this present house will be greater than the glory of the former house,' says the Lord Almighty. 'And in this place I will grant peace,' declares the Lord Almighty."

The prophet Haggai spoke of a time when the heavenly and global systems will be shaken - again. The main purpose is to return glory to God, which belongs to Him. In that process, the "silver and gold" which speaks of economic systems, will also be shaken. It is vital that all believers understand and practice Biblical economic principles, so that when the worldly economic systems are shaken, we will not be affected. Godly principles will always protect and provide for us.

Psalm 91:3-8
³ Surely he will save you from the fowler's snare and from the deadly pestilence.
⁴ He will cover you with his feathers, and under his wings you will find refuge; his faithfulness will be your shield and rampart.
⁵ You will not fear the terror of night, nor the arrow that flies by day,
⁶ nor the pestilence that stalks in the darkness, nor the plague that destroys at midday.
⁷ A thousand may fall at your side, ten thousand at your right hand, but it will not come near you.
⁸ You will only observe with your eyes and see the punishment of the wicked.

The above Psalm speaks of supernatural protection and providence in the midst of deadly pestilence, plague, terror, death and destruction. What keeps us safe in times like this is not natural principles, but supernatural principles. Therefore, as believers, we must train ourselves in financial matters beyond natural management, but rather in supernatural principles. Then we will only observe the destruction around us, while not being harmed by it ourselves.

Philippians 4:10-20
¹⁰ I rejoiced greatly in the Lord that at last you renewed your concern for me. Indeed, you were concerned, but you had no opportunity to show it.
¹¹ I am not saying this because I am in need, for I have learned to be content whatever the circumstances.
¹² I know what it is to be in need, and I know what it is to have

plenty. I have learned the secret of being content in any and every situation, whether well fed or hungry, whether living in plenty or in want.

13 I can do all this through him who gives me strength.

14 Yet it was good of you to share in my troubles.

15 Moreover, as you Philippians know, in the early days of your acquaintance with the gospel, when I set out from Macedonia, not one church shared with me in the matter of giving and receiving, except you only;

16 for even when I was in Thessalonica, you sent me aid more than once when I was in need.

17 Not that I desire your gifts; what I desire is that more be credited to your account.

18 I have received full payment and have more than enough. I am amply supplied, now that I have received from Epaphroditus the gifts you sent. They are a fragrant offering, an acceptable sacrifice, pleasing to God.

19 And my God will meet all your needs according to the riches of his glory in Christ Jesus.

20 To our God and Father be glory for ever and ever. Amen.

Before concluding his letter to the Philippians, Paul thanked them for the gift they sent to him. Many believers quote verse 13 about being able to do all things through Christ. In reality, the context of the entire passage is about being content. Paul knew what it meant to have much, or be in need, and therefore his attitude in both situations was: to be content.

There are times in our life where we may have an abundance - enjoy it. There may be other times in our life where we may be lacking - then learn to be prudent. Joseph was placed in Egypt for that very purpose, to help them manage their crops during the seven years of plenty, so it would outlast them during the seven years of want.

While welcoming their gift, Paul was not expecting it. He was prepared to live with what he had. However, he stated that their gift was a "fragrant offering" or an aroma pleasing to God. It was an "acceptable sacrifice" as it surely cost them something. He said the gift will be "credited" to them as surely, they will reap what they sowed. Besides, he was confident that God will meet all their "needs", not greed. Above all, glory was given to God.

Haggai 1:3-6
³ Then the word of the Lord came through the prophet Haggai:
⁴ "Is it a time for you yourselves to be living in your panelled houses, while this house remains a ruin?"
⁵ Now this is what the Lord Almighty says: "Give careful thought to your ways.
⁶ You have planted much, but harvested little. You eat, but never have enough. You drink, but never have your fill. You put on clothes, but are not warm. You earn wages, only to put them in a purse with holes in it."

We end with a sober warning from Haggai during a time where the people had the power to work, earn wealth, plant, harvest, eat but never seemed satisfied. The wages they earned seemed like it was put in a purse with a hole in it. How ironic? This curse was on them, because they neglected God's house and His blessings were therefore withheld. While we may earn much, if our expenditure is beyond our income, we will still be in want. However, when we put God first, He will help us manage our income, to the point of over-abundance.

Compare that with the children of Israel, who wandered in the desert for 40 years, and had no need for anything. It says in Deuteronomy 29:5-6, "Yet the Lord says, "During the forty years that I led you through the wilderness, your clothes did not wear out, nor did the sandals on your feet. You ate no bread and drank no wine or other fermented drink. I did this so that you might know that I am the Lord your God."

It always fascinates me that their clothes did not wear out, nor did the sandals on their feet. This speaks of God's practical providence down to the tiniest details. Naturally, the size of their clothes let alone sandals must have changed during the 40-year journey in the desert. It is a wonder, how God supernaturally kept them from wearing out. These are signs of supernatural providence.

As we end this book, I appeal to my brothers and sisters, practice all 7 Biblical Economic Principles. Be good stewards of everything God has entrusted you with. Aspire to become a channel of God's blessing to this world. Let your gifts be a fragrant aroma, pleasing to God, and bring glory and honour to Him. While involved and engaged in global economy, do not neglect Biblical Economy. God's principles are eternal, and they work everywhere. May you engage, be involved and practice all 7 Biblical Economic Principles and experience supernatural providence in your storehouse. In the Name of Jesus Christ, I pray. Amen.